ALSO BY KEVIN TACHER

Title Insurance Tips and Secrets!
Learn how to save hundreds of dollars on your next closing

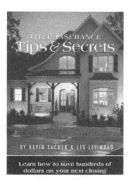

The Little Black Quote Book!
Motivational Quotes and Inspirational Messages from
Key Thought Leaders

SOLD! *(Amazon.com Best-seller)*
The World's Leading Real Estate Experts Reveal the
Secrets to Selling Your Home for Top Dollar in Record Time!

Rescue Your Business! *(Amazon.com Best-seller)*
The Business Strategies of a Firefighter Turned
7 Figure Entrepreneur

The Title Wave of Real Estate

Everything You Need to Know about Title Insurance and Real Estate Closings

By Amazon.com Best-Selling Author
Kevin Tacher

Contributing Author
Alana Burrell

Printed in the United States of America

This publication is designed to provide accurate and authoritative information in regard to the subject matter covered. It is sold with the understanding that the publisher and author are not engaged in rendering legal, accounting, financial, investment, tax or other professional services. If legal advice or other expert assistance is required, the services of a competent professional person should be sought. By reading this publication you agree to hold the author and publisher harmless for any acts that might result as a consequence of reading this book or attending any seminar, workshop or boot camp presented by the author or his associates. Please note that all forms, contracts and documents in this book might not be applicable for your state and should be reviewed by an attorney in your state. Please consult with your attorney, CPA, financial advisor and other professional advisors relating to acting on any information contained in this book.

Published By:

Independence Title, Inc.
4700 West Prospect Road, Suite 115
Fort Lauderdale, Florida 33309

Table of Contents

THE TITLE WAVE OF REAL ESTATE

ABOUT THE AUTHOR

Kevin Tacher – also known as "The Title King" – is the Founder and Chief Executive Officer of Independence Title Inc., a Fort Lauderdale, Florida based title insurance company. Kevin is an amazon.com best-selling author and national real estate speaker. As seen on NBC as well as in person, Kevin has shared the stage with some of the country's best real estate and motivational speakers.

As a trailblazer in the industry, Kevin founded the nationally recognized website TitleRate.com which is the leading source for title insurance rates, real estate mobile applications and up-to-date real estate information. He values community relationships, and is involved with several non-profit organizations across the country. Among his various philanthropic contributions, Kevin and his wife have donated towards reducing the struggles of individuals and families in poverty, preventing child abuse by helping abused and neglected children, as well as supporting our military families in our local community.

Prior to moving to Florida in 2001, Kevin grew up in Long Island, NY where he was a firefighter and Fire Safety Director for the Crowne Plaza Hotel in New York City. He moved to Florida only twenty days before September 11, narrowly missing that tragic event. Professionally, Kevin has worked and held licenses as a mortgage consultant, real estate broker, general lines insurance agent and title insurance agent. Armed with extensive knowledge and experience in the real estate industry, Kevin opened Independence

Title in Fort Lauderdale, Florida. His previous real estate experience enables him to provide a complete range of knowledge for homeowners and real estate professionals throughout the State of Florida. Kevin enjoys scuba diving and fishing. He lives in South Florida with his wife Alana, his daughter Lindsay, his son Jaxon and baby cat Bandito.

You can read more of Kevin's material on his website at: www.TitleRate.com

To learn more about Kevin Tacher, "The Title King," and how you can receive copies of his books, please visit: www.TitleRate.com or call 954-335-9305

CONTRIBUTING AUTHOR

Alana Burrell – was born and raised in Toronto, Canada. She was involved with family businesses her entire life with entrepreneurship in her blood, her ambition lead her to own several businesses, the first at only 18 years old. She has overcome many personal and professional obstacles demonstrating her dynamic and resilient personality. After graduating high school with Honors she went onto study Business Management, specializing in Marketing and Advertising at Seneca College as well as attending Humber Collage for Photography to utilize her creative side while benefiting her love of marketing and advertising. She also studied Events Management at Ryerson University to enhance her knowledge after opening Living the Life Incorporated a company dedicated to coaching, consulting, events and incentives through a belief in creating balance between the way the world is and the way you want it to be.

At 23 years old she was the youngest person ever elected as a Director for the Vaughan Chamber of Commerce and was an instrumental Board member for 4 consecutive years. She was motivated, resourceful and believed actions spoke louder than words and constantly demonstrated those beliefs.

Alana has always believed in her philanthropic endeavors and has been continuously involved local charities, fundraisers and giving back within the community. She thoroughly enjoys volunteering in a variety of organizations and is currently in the process of starting her own in the honor of her mother and grandfather's memories.

Deciding the Canadian winters were no longer for her, she implemented a plan to become a snowbird in 2009. The next season at a Foreclosure Convention she met her Husband Kevin, amazing step-daughter Lindsay then made the move to Florida full time in 2013. However, her wings are not fully clipped, and she still maintains a home in Toronto to visit all her beloved friends and family there!

Alana has always had a love of Real Estate, and completed the Real Estate Licensing program in Toronto, Canada. She is an investor and a Licensed REALTOR in Florida, helping Canadian friends and family with their vacation and investment properties and has been a certified Property Manager since 2009. Over the years, behind the scenes, she helped develop and support her husband's business, has participated in his charitable activities and is grateful they both believe in giving back. They are both very driven and love the wonderful world of Real Estate! She is a dedicated Mother to Jaxon and Step Mother (aka S-mom as her step daughter refers to her) and is committed to be a nurturing role model, teaching them both to fish ~ not just feeding them lunch and feels blessed to have such incredible children in her life.

In her spare time, Alana loves living life to the fullest, travelling, creating memories with friends and family and all things water related. She has been addicted to scuba diving for the last 3 years, logging over 200 dives in over 10 different countries and is always looking for her next adventure both above and below the water!

For more information, feel free to visit www.AlanaBurrell.com or to learn about all things Florida visit at her site at www.SnowbirdSolutions.com or by calling (954) 681.6181.

DEDICATIONS

To my incredible children Lindsay & Jaxon … your growth provides a constant source of joy and pride. I thank you for always making me smile and for understanding when I have to work instead of play. I hope that one day you can read this book and understand why I spent so much time working. May your lives continue to be filled with joyous memories.

To my amazing wife Alana … you were so supportive when my last book came out and have continued to support me through every journey. Without your encouragement, emotional support and great advice, none of this would have been a success. Thank you for contributing to this book in so many ways and I am proud to share its success with you.

To my parents Robert and Maryann … you've supported me throughout my career and it's greatly appreciated. I look forward to being able to share this book with you when it comes out.

To my grandparents Aron and Trudy … you've laid out a path of true financial success for me to shadow and it's greatly treasured.

To my mentors Cyndi and David… thank you for your mentorship throughout the years. Your commitment to today's success has set me on the path for a greater tomorrow.

To my good friends Jim and Lex … if it wasn't for you both, I wouldn't be where I am today. Your support and encouragement is exceptional, and I'm honored to be a part of your world-class team of real estate professionals.

To my entire staff at Independence Title … your dedication and commitment to our mission is greatly appreciated and I thank you for being part of our amazing team of title professionals.

SPECIAL DEDICATION

I would like to make a special dedication to
my mother-in-law Eileen Burrell and father-in-law Kenneth Burrell.
Your kindness and devotion to your family will never be forgotten.
I will always remember
how you displayed my last book so proudly in your office.
I know you are both following our journey
and always looking over us.
You are greatly missed but will never be forgotten.

PREFACE

This book was written as the result of over thirteen years of thought, research, and experience in the South Florida Real Estate market. I've been in the title insurance industry for many years and have seen a wide array of transactions go smoothly. I've also seen my fair share of transactions that *didn't* go as well. All in all, I've closed over three thousand five hundred transactions in my career as a Florida licensed title insurance agent, and I like to think that I've seen just about everything when it comes to buying and selling real estate in South Florida.

Amongst the many real estate transactions for title insurance that go smoothly when purchasing and/or selling a property, there are also some incidences of fraud. In my years of experience, I've seen quite a fair share of these incidences. Imagine this scenario: a man posed as the owner of a piece of property who came to the title company to close the sale of the property. The man had picture identification in the name of the owner of the property and even showed up with an attorney he had retained to represent him in the transaction. Due to an issue with the buyer's financing, the closing did not occur, but the man had a back-up contract, which he closed at another title agent's office. When the real owner discovered someone else living in his property, he was understandably upset, as was the title insurance company that was hit with a claim for the complete failure of title to the property.

When it comes to buying and selling real estate, people want to know that they are dealing with honest people. My company *Independence Title*, was founded many years ago with a mission to be the most efficient title company in the industry. It's been my ongoing objective to surpass the standards of service previously offered within the title company ranks. We constantly accomplish this by establishing strong relationships with proven strategic alliances, offering competitive pricing, and delivering a satisfying experience, by both anticipating the needs and exceeding the expectations of our clients.

We've also developed the nationally recognized website TitleRate.com to help expand learning opportunities for individuals interested in real estate. Our principle is clear and simple: *Clients interested in real estate should be equipped with all of the tools, strategies, and education necessary to help them achieve great success in their careers, while keeping their titles well protected.*

I wrote this book with that same mission in mind: to give the readers tips, suggestions, and educational nuggets that will make a difference in the way they close their next real estate transaction.

If your title is well inspected, your investment is protected.

Chapter 1

Introduction to Title Insurance

"A broker was dismayed when a brand new real estate office much like his own opened next door and erected a huge sign reading 'BEST AGENTS.' He was horrified when another competitor opened up on his right, and announced its arrival with an even larger sign, LOWEST COMMISSIONS. The broker panicked, until he got an idea. He put the biggest sign of all over his own real estate office. It read: 'MAIN ENTRANCE'"

(Source: http://www.xcaliburtitle.com/IndustryHumor.htm)

The business of real estate is just that, a business; it is a business for people and about people. Title insurance is a part of that business. Before we get into the details of title insurance, I'd like to introduce you to some history and background. If you're going to move forward, you need to know exactly what title insurance *is*.

Title insurance is the amount of insurance that you have covering your real estate transaction. It's usually the amount of the purchase price, and protects the owner of the property – as well as the lender's financial interest in the property – against loss due to defects in title, liens, judgments, unrecorded liens, code enforcement violations, city liens, unpaid water bills, and other problems.

Title insurance is issued in the United States upon the purchase of real property. Issuance of this title insurance policy ensures that you have a clear and marketable title to a property when you purchase it. This insurance has many facets, including lien searches, title commitments, title policies, etc., which we'll be discussing in further detail throughout this book. Essentially, title insurance is insurance that protects you and your property.

Unique only to the US, title insurance came about due to the deficiency of the US land record laws, which did not protect a purchaser of real property from title defects in the past. This became evident in 1868, after a court case where the plaintiff lost his investment due a previous lien on the property – which had been deemed invalid by the attorney of the defendant – in error. The courts ruled in favor of the defendant, stating that he and others in similar situations weren't liable for mistakes derived from professional opinion.

On 28th March, 1876, a group of Philadelphia-based conveyances incorporated the first ever title insurance company, in response to this situation. Their aim was to:

> Insure the purchasers of real estate and mortgages against losses from defective titles, liens and encumbrances," and that "through these facilities, the transfer of real estate and real estate securities can be made more speedily and with greater security than heretofore.

Title insurance only insures the past. The purpose of title insurance is to protect a buyer of a property and to ensure that prior to the purchase, all outstanding liens, judgments, etc., attached to that property are satisfied or resolved. It's to protect the buyer from things that *have* happened to the property, rather than things that *will* happen.

Once these outstanding items are resolved, the title will be considered clear and marketable, meaning the property can be sold. The title company then issues a title insurance policy that outlines specifically the amount of title insurance the policy covers – usually the purchase price or the amount of the loan that is secured and recorded against the property.

It is possible to buy real estate without a title policy, but to do so would be extremely foolish, since it would expose the buyer to any problems that occurred with that property before they purchased it. Some wholesale real estate investors try to save money by not getting title insurance. This is a big mistake. You should always get title insurance, even if you're doing a simultaneous or double closing, since you want the end buyer to be protected as much as the first buyer on the first transaction.

Florida's regulation of title insurance is guided by state law, administrative rules, and judicial decisions. Until January 2003, the Department of Insurance regulated Florida's title insurance industry. As part of the 2002 Cabinet reorganization, the Legislature gave the Department of Financial Services the responsibility of regulating title insurance agents and agencies. The Legislature specifically assigned the Office of Insurance Regulation the responsibility of regulating title insurance companies. This divided oversight of the title insurance industry creates challenges related to standards for agent licensing and oversight, rate setting, and payment of the title insurance premium tax. These are now challenges that real estate professionals need to understand and deal with, if they want to be successful.

Title insurance also protects a property owner or lender against loss in the event of dispute or discrepancy over property ownership rights. It's a monoline product, which means that insurers selling title insurance cannot sell other types of insurance products. Industry analysts suggest that this fact makes the industry susceptible to more volatility and dependence on regional and national economic conditions, and this may be true. In Florida and across the country, title insurance is highly concentrated. Nationally, only 5 insurers account for 92 percent of the business. This means that those five insurers are responsible for a very large amount of title insurance across the nation, so that the state of any title insurance depends on their economic success. For that reason, it's incredibly important to understand their processes – and the nationwide trends for title insurance – if you're to protect yourself, your clients, and your properties.

History of Title Insurance

To understand title insurance we must understand its history. Title assurance systems in America were derived from the English conveyance system, which relied on attorneys, known as conveyancers, to search out private documents, since there were no public documents to determine the condition of a title. Over time, the American system developed four additional mechanisms for guaranteeing title to real estate:

- *Title Abstracts, which provide a permanent record of a title search*

- *Title Certificates, which combine the title search and the opinion of the title*

- *Title Insurance, which affords protection against errors in the conveyance process*

- *Land Registration Systems, which rely on judicial proceedings to convey title assurance*

Collectively, these mechanisms rely on researching the chronological ownership of property to identify recorded events that have contributed to a title's present condition. This ownership history is then evaluated in light of legal decisions and the requirements demanded by the real estate investment community.

After World War II, title insurance became a national standard for the real estate industry. Institutional lenders required borrowers to use title insurance services to guarantee clear title to property as a condition of purchasing mortgage loans. From there, Florida's title insurance industry went through several historical regulatory benchmarks. The title insurance industry's development in Florida is tied to statutory and administrative law, as well as key judicial decisions. Prior to 1954, only attorneys could process title transfers and issue opinions on the status of property titles. Insurers then issued policies based on these opinions.

However, in 1954, the Florida Supreme Court ruled in the Cooperman case that corporations could issue title policies and supervise property transfers, holding that these activities did not constitute the practice of law, and thus could not be limited to attorneys. The Legislature recognized and defined title insurance in 1959. In 1965, it went on to give the insurance commissioner authority to promulgate rates for title insurance premiums.

This established the foundation for the state's current regulation of title insurance, as much of the statutory history of title insurance relates to regulation of rates and establishing the qualifications and procedures for licensing and monitoring agents and insurers. In 1992, the Legislature mandated the licensing of title agents and agencies, unless the agents were direct employees of a registered title insurance company.

The most recent significant change concerning title insurance regulation occurred in 2002, when voters passed a constitutional amendment to create the position of Chief Financial Officer. At that time, as part of the cabinet reform initiative, the Legislature eliminated the Departments of Insurance and Banking and Finance, and created the Department of Financial Services and the Financial Services Commission. The Department of Financial Services operates under the Chief Financial Officer. The Insurance Commissioner and the Office of Insurance Regulation are administratively housed in the department, and operate under the

Financial Services Commission, but are not directly under the authority of the Chief Financial Officer. This means that all title insurance responsibilities are housed in the same departments for better efficiency and tracking.

Components of Title Insurance

When you're working with a title company or attorney for your real estate closing, there are many items related to the settlement of your purchase or sale of residential property. The main items are as follows:

- Title Insurance Policy
- Title Insurance Commitment
- Title Search
- Title Examination
- Municipal City/County Lien Search
- Closing Costs
- HUD-1 Settlement Statement
- Inspection Reports
- City/County Property Taxes
- Boundary Survey
- Homeowners and Flood Insurance
- Mortgages

With these components and procedures in place, title companies work to provide comprehensive title insurance to homebuyers, as well as assisting many real estate professionals and investors in completing their closing.

To protect yourself, it's imperative that you hire a reputable, experienced title company, like Independence Title (www.TitleRate.com) to deal with your title insurance needs. Hiring a professional who knows what they're talking about means better protection for you and the property. Going through the process without a professional, and without proper education, may open you up to fraudulent individuals.

Title Insurance in Action

The Title policy is a policy issued by the insurance company indicating what is and what isn't covered. It's the next step in the insuring process. Before you can get a title policy, though, you need a title commitment.

The Title commitment is issued by the closing agent before the closing takes place, and tells you what will and will not be covered in your final title policy. The final title policy is issued at closing, and is based on the information contained in the title commitment.

It's important to remember that title insurance protects the owner and/or lender from defects that

Essentially, title insurance is insurance that protects you and your title.

arise prior to the date of purchase or closing. It's not like traditional insurance, which protects you moving forward after the purchase of a property. This means that if any liens are placed on the property after you take ownership, they won't be covered by your current title insurance policy. If, for example, you hired a contractor and didn't pay them in full, they could place a lien on your property for the amount still owing. This lien would be made after the date of the title policy we covered above, so you would need to remove this cloud on the title before you could sell the property.

If, however, an old lien was somehow missed during a title search, and eventually surfaces, the new owner and/or lender is fully protected from that lien by the current title insurance policy.

Home ownership represents the biggest financial obligation most people will incur in their lifetime. In fact, home ownership is considered to be a fundamental part of wealth building. During the home buying process, and particularly during closing, many of us are faced with a barrage of terms and procedures we've never heard of, especially if we're first-time home buyers. The closing process is often shrouded in mystery, and many homebuyers face it with only a minimal understanding of what will happen, or what their rights and obligations are.

In Florida, your closing transaction will typically be handled by a title insurance agent or real estate attorney. In addition to ensuring that title insurance is purchased, your title insurance agent or attorney will facilitate the entire closing process. They hold any funds, such as earnest money deposits, in escrow until they're disbursed. But who are these professionals, and what exactly are their responsibilities? What is your role as the homebuyer or seller? And, most importantly, how can you save money in this process? Now that we know what title insurance is and the role it plays in the closing, let's move forward with an overview of the costs and terms of title insurance.

Chapter 2

Closing Costs

When you've bought or sold a property it doesn't just stop at the price of the property. There are more fees to be paid. The various fees involved in the closing of a real estate transaction are called the closing costs. At the time that a real estate contract is signed, the buyer should be provided with an information sheet describing the fees that will be associated with the transaction. This includes estimates for routine inspections, that are performed as part of the sales process, along with the closing costs such as the recording fee and loan origination fee. It's important to be aware that these are only estimates, and that the closing costs may be lower or higher than predicted, depending on a number of factors.

Buyers who are concerned about closing costs can discuss the possibility of asking the seller to pay these costs. Some sellers will agree to this in exchange for a slightly higher sales price or as a concession to a qualified buyer. Generally in a so-called "seller's market," buyers will not be able to obtain such concessions from sellers, but when buyers have the advantage; it may be possible to negotiate. Closing costs may include:

- **Application Fee**
If there is a mortgage, the lender (bank) can charge an application fee, which can cost anywhere from $50 to $700.
- **Underwriting Fees**
This is the fee charged by the lender who is approving you for a loan.

- **Flood Certificate Fee**

This fee is charged by the lender to determine if the property is in a FEMA flood hazard zone. If it is, then an elevation certificate or proof of flood insurance will be required.

- **Tax Service Fee**

This is the fee that the lender charges to ensure that property taxes are paid on the property each year that the loan is in place.

- **Loan Origination Fee**

This is what the lender charges you as an up-front fee when they give you the loan which is usually paid at closing.

- **Loan Discount Fee**

This is the fee that the lender charges for reducing the interest rate on the loan.

- **Document Preparation Fee**

This is the fee charged by the lender for preparing the loan documents.

- **Escrow Account**

Most lenders require you to escrow money in advance for property taxes and property insurance. This amount could be equal to up to fourteen months of payments.

- **Prepaid Interest**

If your closing takes place between the first and the fifth day of the month, then you will receive a credit for the five days and your first payment will be due on the first day of the next month. If you close after the fifth day of the month, then you will be charged the remaining days of interest for the remainder of the month, and your first payment will be due the first day of the following month (not the next month).

- **Settlement Fee**

This is the closing cost charged by the title company or the real estate attorney that is handling the closing.

- **Title Search**

This is the charge by the title company for performing the title search.

- **Title Insurance**

You have to have title insurance to close if there is a mortgage and lender involved. Cash transactions do not require title insurance, but you should always pay for a title insurance policy even if you aren't required to have one. If you qualify for a reissue credit, then the title insurance premium will be substantially reduced. It is typical in Broward or Miami-Dade Counties for the buyer to pay for title insurance and to choose the title agent. In the rest of the state of Florida, it's customary for the seller to pay for title and to choose the title agent.

- **Intangible Taxes**

This is .0020 percent of the loan amount charged by state of Florida at closing.

- **Document Stamps New Mortgage**

This is $0.35/ $100 for new money (borrowed money), such as a mortgage. This is a mandatory charge, and is charged by the state of Florida.

- **Document Stamps Deed**

The seller is charged $0.70/ $100 on the sale price of the transaction. This is a mandatory charge, and is charged by the state of Florida.

There can also be other fees, such as postage, notary, copy, courier, etc. Many of these fees are negotiable and sometimes can be reduced. This is how your title company pads up your closing costs. Florida title insurance rates are governed by what is known as the promulgated rate, which is the rate recommended by the state.

The **Promulgated Rate** for a title insurance policy in Florida is as follows:

- $5.75 per $1,000 of real estate value up to $100,000
- $5.00 per $1,000 of real estate value up to $1,000,000
- $2.50 per $1,000 of real estate value up to $5,000,000
- $2.25 per $1,000 of real estate value up to $10,000,000

There are plenty of fees that you'll have to pay for during the closing. Depending on prior negotiations, the buyer or the seller could be responsible for these costs, although typically the most of it is paid by the buyer.

All closing costs are spelled out in the lender's good faith estimate. If you want to make sure that you're paying the least amount possible in closing cost fees, you should get at least three **good faith estimates** from mortgage lenders. Keep in mind that this is only an estimate, and the actual charges may differ. RESPA allows the borrower to request to see the HUD-1 settlement statement, which shows all actual charges imposed on borrower in connection with the settlement one day before the settlement. If you see a charge that doesn't make sense, or that no other lender has, it's time to ask questions.

In addition to the sales price of the home, there are a variety of costs associated with finalizing the transaction. Those fees are featured below:

Real Estate Broker Commission/Fees (Section 700)

If you use a real estate agent to help you buy your home, the cost of the agent's services can be paid in one of two ways. Generally, the seller pays for all agents in a transaction in an amount usually stated as a percentage of the sales price. While this amount will be deducted – along with other seller-paid closing costs – from any amount the seller might otherwise be paid, and is usually stated on the HUD-1, it will not be your charge. Increasingly, buyers are engaging their own so-called "buyer's broker or agent."

Loan Fees – Direct Loan Costs (Section 800)

Most people need to obtain a mortgage loan to pay for their home. There are often fees associated with obtaining a loan such as the ones listed below.

- **Loan Origination Fee**
This fee covers the lender's cost of obtaining financing and administration for your loan. It's usually calculated as a percentage of the loan amount, but can also be a flat dollar amount. It has become more common to add an "application" fee (stated in flat dollar amount) and, possibly, other up-front charges like an "underwriting" fee (also usually in flat dollar terms), either to take the place of or be in addition to an origination fee. Each lender and loan program a lender offers will have different front-end charges. You should shop carefully and examine all the fees and terms prior to closing. It is generally too late to change those fees and terms at closing.
- **Loan Discount Fee** (Sometimes referred to as "points")
This is a one-time fee charged by the lender in order to give you a lower interest rate on your loan. Each point is 1 percent of the mortgage amount. Points paid up front can reduce the interest rate you pay on your loan. Whether this is the best option for you in shopping for a mortgage loan depends on whether you have the necessary cash, and how long you think you'll stay in the home or keep the mortgage before selling or refinancing. The longer you intend to stay and keep the financing, the better off you may bc paying something upfront in exchange for a lower interest rate on your loan. In any event, this cost will be collected at closing, generally.

- **Appraisal Fees**

To approve your loan, your lender has to obtain an estimate of what your home is really worth. The appraisal fee covers the cost of getting an estimate of the market value of your home, usually by an independent, certified, licensed appraiser.

- **Credit Report Fee**

Mortgage lenders require a credit report to determine whether or not you're eligible (have good enough credit) for a loan, how much they will lend you, and at what interest rate. Credit reports today often also include a "credit score," which is an indicator of your history of ability and willingness to repay the loan. The higher your credit score, the better risk you are.

- **Lender Inspection Fees**

If the lender requires certain inspections to take place before closing (particularly where new construction or recent repairs are involved), such inspection fees, payable to the lender or its designee, will appear in this section of the HUD-1.

- **Mortgage Insurance Application Fee**

There are often fees associated with processing an application for mortgage insurance. Some private mortgage insurers waive the application fee. This line of the HUD-1 may be used for other fees when the borrower is seeking an FHA-insured or VA-guaranteed loan.

- **Assumption Fee**

If you're taking over the existing mortgage loan on the home, there is often a charge associated with assuming the mortgage, called the assumption fee.

- **Mortgage Broker Fee**

This fee covers the costs of services of a mortgage broker if you engage one to help you shop for mortgage financing. Mortgage brokers typically present the borrower's application to a variety of funding sources before helping the borrower make their final selection.

- **Yield Spread Premium (YSP)**

This is a fee that the funding lender may pay directly to the mortgage broker or other third-party loan originator. This fee is for securing a borrower on behalf of the funding lender at rate and terms agreed upon, which may be higher than what is called "at par." The fee is sometimes called a "par-plus pricing" fee. While this fee is not paid by the borrower (it is typically shown as "POC" by the lender), it must be shown on the HUD-1 if the mortgage broker is receiving such compensation.

Items Required by the Lender to Be Paid in Advance (Section 900)

There are certain items the lender may require you to pay at the time of closing. These could include:

- **Interest**

Lenders usually require payment of loan interest from and including the day of closing through the end of the month of closing. After that, interest is accrued and paid as part of the monthly loan instalments.

- **Mortgage Insurance Premium**

At the settlement, you may be required to pay your first year's mortgage insurance premium, or a lump sum premium that covers the life of the loan. This fee is payable to a private mortgage insurance company. If the loan is being federally insured (FHA) or guaranteed (VA), the mortgage insurance or funding fees for those government loan programs would be charged here.

- **Hazard Insurance Premium**

Oftentimes lenders require payment of one year's hazard insurance, commonly referred to as homeowner's insurance, against fire, windstorms, and natural hazards. In order to bind the coverage, the premium is often paid in advance of closing.

- **Flood Insurance**

Depending on the location of your home, flood insurance may be required and payment of the first year's premium must be made in advance of closing.

Escrows/Impounds/Reserves (Section 1000)

Although the lender isn't required to provide an estimate of the reserves they'll be collecting, it is important that you be aware of whether the lender will or will not be "escrowing" for taxes, mortgage insurance (if any), hazard, and flood insurance. The use of an escrow/impound account to build up the funds needed to pay these items as they become due can often be a good way for borrowers to budget, rather than having to pay these large sums out-of-pocket when they come due. Be sure to ask your lender in advance of closing how these items will be paid on a go-forward basis.

Title and Closing Charges (Section 1100)

These fees cover the administrative costs of a title search, title examination, issuance of the title commitment/binder, and final title insurance policy(ies.) Also included would be charges for conducting the closing/settlement/escrow. You are free to select the company to conduct your closing/settlement/escrow, and to shop for the best pricing. Title and closing charges may include:

- **Settlement/Closing Fee**

A fee must be paid to a settlement agent who has prepared documents, calculated figures, and overseen proper execution of closing documents. This fee is often split between buyer and seller, but can be negotiated as part of the sales contract.

- **Abstract of Title, Search, Title Examination, Title Insurance Commitment or Binder**

In order to ensure that there are no pre-existing problems with your property, a title insurance professional must perform a title search and produce documentation on the homes title history. In some places, one or more of these charges will appear separately on the HUD-1, while in other places, they may be included within the title insurance premium. When a mortgage loan is involved, there may also be added charges for special endorsements, which will accompany the lender's title policy.

- **Document Preparation**

Some settlement agents charge for the cost of preparing legal papers such as the mortgage, deed of trust, note or deed, and/or other loan and title documentation. If a lender charges a document preparation fee, it will typically appear in the Loan Fees/Direct Loan Costs section of the HUD-1.

- **Notary Fee**

Because there are legal documents involved, a licensed notary is required to acknowledge the fact that the proper people signed these official documents in their presence. Notaries usually charge a fee for their services.

- **Attorney Fees**

Both the homebuyer and the seller might have their own legal representation to prepare and record legal documents. Frequently, however, where an attorney is acting as a settlement agent, there may only be one involved in the closing. Who pays for those services is a matter of contract negotiation, but is often handled like fees paid to any other settlement agent/title agent.

- **Title Insurance**

There are two kinds of title insurance policies: loan and owner's policies. The cost for the loan policy is based on the loan amount, and the cost for the owner's policy is based on the sales price of the home. Who pays these one-time fees at closing varies from state to state. Ask your settlement agent how it's handled in your area. In some circumstances, discounts may be available (such as a "reissue rate" or "reissue credit") when the property has recently been insured by a title insurer. Be sure to ask whether you're entitled to any discounts.

Recording/Government Filing Fees (Section 1200)

Buying a home is not only a big investment; it's also a matter of public record. The property information and loan information are required to be filed at the county courthouse or other local government recording office. Filing fees include:

- **Recording Fees**
  The recording fee is paid to a government body, which enters an official record of the change of ownership.
- **Transfer Taxes, Document or Transaction Stamps**
  These are government charges based on the amount of the mortgage and, often, also on the purchase price. Depending on your location, there could be a city, county, or state tax involved, or some combination of these.

To be more specific, a recording fee or administration fee is a fee charged by a government agency to record the details of a real estate sale or deed. These details must be recorded in the public record, and the recording fee is included in the closing costs for a sale along with a number of related fees. After closing, people should confirm that the change of ownership has been recorded and that the details are correct, as errors may cause problems in the future, most particularly when the property is sold or transferred to someone else.

The amount of a recording fee varies. Government offices that record deeds usually provide a fee schedule for the various services they provide, including recording, making duplicate copies of the title, and looking up records. People can request copies of these fee schedules from staff, and if the government office has a website, this information may be available there as well. Some government offices even provide recording fee calculators for convenience, and title companies may provide such services as well.

Other Miscellaneous Charges (Section 1300)

- **Survey Fee**

Lenders and title insurers often require a surveyor to conduct a survey of the property to define the property size and boundaries. They also verify if any part of the building or other improvements are encroaching on a neighbor's yard or the other way around. They are also looking to see if there are any setback violations or other material matters that are considered problematic.

- **Inspection Fees**

When homes are sold, an inspection is often recommended, and in some cases the contract may even be contingent upon an acceptable inspection report. This fee covers the cost of an inspector checking the dwelling for any structural problems or issues. This is frequently a sales contract term imposed by the homebuyer to obtain an accurate assessment of the condition of the property. The work is done prior to closing, and the fee is often collected at the time of inspection. There are several other inspections that a future homeowner might want to request and a lender might require. These could include pest inspections (termites and other wood-destroying organisms), lead paint inspections (for structures built before 1978), roof inspections, water/well certifications, structural or mechanical inspections, or additional specific inspections based on the property type and location.

Fees for title insurance policies are often the largest component of the closing costs for homebuyers. A standard policy, though, protects the insured against any of the many title problems that can hinder the transfer of a property.

Chapter 3

Title Insurance Cost, Rates, Terms, and Title Agents

Individuals pay for title insurance as a one-time fee at the time of the sale, with the buyer and/or seller paying for the owner's and/or loan policies as a condition of the sale. The premium amount typically depends on the property's sale price in the case of the owner's policy, and the loan amount in the case of the lender's or mortgagee policy. The total cost to the consumer for title insurance also depends on the extent that other costs are included or not included along with the title insurance premium.

In Florida, the premium price depends on the rate in administrative rule, also called the **promulgated rate**, at the time. Along with the premium, the consumer often pays for the title search, as well as services like recording the deed and escrow disbursement. These charges are known as "closing services," and are not included in the premium for title insurance.

Regulatory experts agree that due to limited knowledge of title insurance and limited market competition, consumers generally don't make informed choices about title insurance when purchasing property. Usually someone else involved in the transaction, such as the real estate agent or the lender, recommends a title company, local agency, or law firm. Consumers often pay little attention to the cost of title insurance or related charges, as they don't know much about it. This is something that needs to change, however, if consumers are going to protect themselves.

To establish rates for premium prices, for example, the Florida Department of Insurance office requires agents and insurers to submit statistical information regarding their business operations and current and expected expenses for handling risks. Using this information, the office seeks to determine a reasonable underwriting profit margin and contingencies to allow insurers, agents, and agencies to earn enough profit to attract insurers to the state.

A 1992 study reported that the target profit margin for the industry was 12 percent. The state used this information to establish title insurance rates. However, since 1992, the Office of Insurance Regulation and its predecessor, the Department of Insurance, have been unable to collect sufficient information to revise title insurance rates. The state has issued four requests to agents, insurers, and attorneys to voluntarily submit statistical data (i.e., data calls). These information requests have met with varying degrees of success, but have been hampered by low response rates. The office attributes the low response rate to the nature, extent, and complexity of the requested business operations information.

In 1999, the Legislature froze title insurance rates at the 1992 level for three years. Rates have continued at this level, as the state lacks the statistical data needed to determine whether they're representative of the costs to provide title insurance in 2008. There is a growing need to re-examine the 1992 rates, given changes since that time. While rates have remained constant, housing prices in Florida, on which the title insurance costs are based, have increased 321 percent from 1980 to 2008. As a result, title insurance premiums paid by homeowners have increased substantially, without the homeowners being involved in the process. Together, these changes create a highly volatile environment for title insurance and highlight the need to ensure that consumers pay fair and equitable rates for title insurance. Consumers have a responsibility to learn about these processes and ask the right questions to protect themselves.

Title insurance is the first step in this education for protection. Title

Consumers often pay little attention to the cost of title insurance or related charges, as they don't know much about it.

insurance emphasizes loss prevention by eliminating risks caused by title problems arising from past events. According to the American Land Title Association (ALTA) approximately 25 percent of all residential real estate transactions have issues with the title that are resolved by title professionals before closing. This emphasis on loss prevention results in fewer claims paid by title insurers compared to other lines of insurance. However, loss prevention and clearing title issues is a labor-intensive and costly component of a title company's operating budget. To compare, ALTA also states that the expense ratio for title insurers averages 90 percent, while the expense ratio for property and casualty companies is less than 30 percent.

Knowing about these title issues, proper escrow procedures, closing costs, and choosing the right company will limit the percent of title problems in the future as well as save you money along the way.

Rate Terminology

Here are some terms that you should know when talking to a title company or real estate attorney. Ask your closing agent whether you qualify for any of the following:

- **Reissue Rate**

The reduced rate for an Owner's Policy issued on a property that was previously insured within some period of years. In some states, the term is also used for a refinance rate (see below).

- **Simultaneous Issue Rate**

The reduced rate for a Loan or Owner's Policy issued on a property or loan at the same time as another policy. The term usually refers to a Loan Policy issued at the same time as an Owner's Policy when a property is purchased.

- **Refinance Rate**

The reduced rate for a Loan Policy issued on the new loan in a refinance transaction, in which the original loan was previously insured within some period of years.

Monoline Insurance

The word "monoline" refers to the statutory restriction of companies writing a particular line of insurance. This restriction allows them to write only that line. Enforced at the state level, monoline restrictions currently apply to title insurance, mortgage guaranty insurance, and financial guaranty insurance.

Monoline restrictions allow an insurer to isolate its surplus for the protection of its policyholders. This is important, because the term covered by the single premium collected for a title insurance policy is the duration of property ownership, or the term of the real estate loan. The failure of a title insurance company would affect all its title insurance customers for decades past.

This is important security for both professionals and consumers. The experience of the 1980s showed that periods of financial instability and plunging real estate prices were not a one-time Depression-Era occurrence. Writing title insurance in conjunction with mortgage guaranty insurance would put title insurers and their policyholders at risk, as would insuring irresponsibly. It's important, therefore, to regulate who can write title insurance and how.

Non-title insurance companies – companies that specialize in other high-risk lines – have attempted to offer title insurance products in the past. These companies have no title insurance underwriting experience, and have a much lower aggregate surplus than the title insurance industry. They are therefore unable to assure the policyholders' safety, and cannot deliver the same quality of product as a title insurer. They are not a good choice for title insurance, and should be avoided.

The American Land Title Association (ALTA) believes the monoline restriction for title insurance continues to constitute sound economic and regulatory policy, and encourages this restriction for the safety of everyone concerned. When you're shopping for real estate professionals, make sure you use these recommendations to protect yourself.

Title Agents

Life is filled with many choices, and title agents are no exception. A licensed title agent works for one company and should always be your personal choice. His or her roles and responsibilities are as follows:

- Obtain title searches
- Examine title
- Prepare closing documents
- Prepare and issue title insurance
- Conduct closings
- Disburse closing funds

The role of the title agency is obviously pivotal to your home purchase. But how should you go about selecting a reputable title agent? We'll discuss several tips throughout this book, including what the title agent should do for you.

Opinion of Title

Title companies and title insurance companies rely on licensed attorneys to write what's called an opinion of title, in order to issue a title or insure a title for a property. This document expresses the signatory attorney's opinion regarding the validity of the title, based on research, investigation, and examination of all relevant documentation. Also referred to as a statement of opinion or a title abstract, the document will specify all research conducted by the attorney, name all documentation he or she has looked at, and record any claims or liens found against the title. Upon completion of the opinion of title, a title insurance company can insure the document for the marketer or holder of the title. While state law often specifies the exact information required on the document, most will follow a similar format.

Beginning with a disclaimer informing the reader of the document that the intent or purpose is for decision-making in relation to title insurance or title issuance, but in no way constitutes any sort of obligation on the part of the attorney or company. Thereafter, the attorney will specify the time and date of document completion, as well as the time and date when he or she examined all relevant documents. On the next line, he or she will record the name and location of the property, the type of deed held on the property, and the location of where the deed is recorded.

In the next couple of sections, the attorney will record any liens held on the property and all information associated with identifying the lien holder as having a right over the property. Additionally, the attorney will record the assignees of the lien and all information associated with identifying the assignees. If there are any other claims legally attached to the property, he or she will record them as well.

The licensed title agent represents the real estate closing in an arm's length manner. This is important because their role is to protect the transaction, which in turn protects the buyer, seller and the lender. A licensed title insurance agency is a true free-market player and has the highest incentive to close the deal in a timely and compliant fashion, backed by courteous professional service.

Chapter 4

Different Types of Insurance

Title insurance differs from other forms of insurance in several respects, including scope of coverage, policy term, and level of competition. Two key differences between title insurance and property and casualty insurance are related to the role of the agents and the role of risk.

For most types of insurance, the agent acts as a salesperson and assists the purchaser with forms and applications, while the insurance company's underwriters make the determination and commit the insurer to providing the policy. In contrast, title insurers authorize title agents, based on their review, to make the final decision to provide coverage.

Florida is considered a non-inclusive rate state because the costs of related title services such as title search and closing services are not included in the premium. However, even all-inclusive states differ in what they charge in a premium authority to the agent, and as a result, title agents are often compared to insurance underwriters.

Title insurance also differs from other types of insurance in regards to the amount of risk that the insurer undertakes upon execution of the policy. For example, property and casualty insurers determine the probability of future loss based on the characteristics of the insured party. In contrast, title underwriters focus on reducing the possibility of loss by discovering as much information as possible about the past ownership of a property before the insurance is written. As a result, the title policy does not cover discrepancies or defects in the ownership of the property that occur after the policy's effective date. Let's take a look at some of the differences between title insurance versus other insurances.

Title Insurance versus Homeowner Insurance

Homeowners insurance and title insurance are two totally different types of insurance coverage, each protecting against different risks. Homeowners insurance covers loss or damage to your home, other structures on your property, personal property kept in your home, loss of use, liability, and medical expenses for accidents that occur on your property. Title insurance, on the other hand, protects your ownership in the real property. Title insurance guarantees that you have true entitlement to the property. Many lenders will require you to carry title insurance, so they know for sure that you have clear ownership of the property and the home.

A title insurance company will conduct research before a loan is approved, and search for any outstanding liens, encumbrances, or other defects that may hinder the property ownership from becoming solely yours. Once the title insurance company is sure that that property does not hold any such liens, it will issue title insurance. This protects the owner from anyone else trying to claim ownership of the property.

Additionally, when title insurance is purchased at the closing of a real estate transaction, the property owner has the opportunity to purchase an owner's policy as well. It is financially prudent to get your owner's title policy at the same time the lender's title policy is issued, for two reasons. The first reason is that a substantial discount is given by virtue of the simultaneous issue. Because two policies are being issued at the same time or "simultaneously," the second policy is issued for a minimal flat fee (normally $25.00 in the State of Florida). The second reason is that you save the cost of another title search, which you would incur if you decide to buy a policy at a later date.

Title Insurance versus Mortgage Insurance

Title insurance policies are written to cover a specific tract of land, and can be offered to either the mortgage lender (called a lender's policy) or the purchaser of the property (called an owner's policy). They are usually paid out of closing costs. Title insurance protects against any hidden defects in the title to the property that would not be disclosed by a search of the public records. These include, but are not limited to, a forgery of an earlier transfer document, a missing heir of a previous owner suddenly appearing to claim an interest, or human error in indexing the records. Most mortgage lenders will require a title insurance policy, and will pass the cost on to their borrower.

Owner's policies are usually optional, but highly recommended, as they require only a low one-time payment and can prevent potential attorneys' fees and other costs, in a dollar amount up to the purchase price of the property. The insurance policy will protect an insured owner for life, even after he or she moves away from the property.

Mortgage insurance policies are written to cover a specific loan, solely to protect a mortgage lender in the case the borrower defaults and does not make his/her payments, so that the lender must foreclose.

This policy is most often required when the borrower does not have enough "ownership" in the value of the house relative to the loan amount. The typical requirement is at least 80 percent equity, which for a buyer translates to a 20 percent or higher down payment. It allows a buyer that normally would not have enough cash for a down payment to acquire a loan, or an owner to obtain a loan to refinance property, even if that property does not yet have enough equity in the home to obtain a loan on its own.

The conventional belief of financial institutions is that the less a borrower feels they have invested in the house, the more likely they are to "walk away." The mortgage insurance is meant to make up the difference in the debt-to-equity ratio. It, too, is a cost passed along to the borrower, but as part of the monthly mortgage payment. With loans insured by the Federal Housing Administration (FHA) program, an up-front mortgage insurance payment is also required, usually about 3 percent of the loan amount, paid at closing.

Mortgage insurance is an insurance policy that protects a mortgage lender in the event that the borrower defaults on payments, dies, or is otherwise unable to meet the contractual obligations of the mortgage. This can refer to private mortgage insurance (PMI), mortgage life insurance, or mortgage title insurance. What these have in common is an obligation to make the lender or property holder whole in the event of specific cases of loss.

Private mortgage insurance may be called "lender's mortgage insurance" (LMI) if the premium on a PMI policy is paid by the lender rather than the borrower. This is typically done in exchange for a higher rate or fee structure on the mortgage itself.

When a mortgage is purchased, the homeowner may have an option to cover their insurance with a payment plan or a lump sum payment. Homeowners who are required to have PMI because of the 80 percent loan-to-value ratio rule can request that the insurance policy be canceled once 20 percent of the principal balance has been paid off.

Covering Secondary Mortgages

The nationwide growth of a secondary mortgage market began in the mid-1940s, and has proved to be an especially dramatic benefit for millions of American homebuyers.

Essentially, the purpose of the secondary market is to broaden the base of investment for mortgage financing and attract funds from areas of the country with abundant capital to areas where mortgage money is needed. Unlike the New York Stock Exchange and other organized trading markets, where representatives of buyers and sellers meet in a single location, the secondary market consists of a complex network of organizations, intermediaries, and various channels of communication. Through this facility, lenders in one area of the country with funds to invest can readily make or purchase mortgage loans on real property located elsewhere.

Secondary market operations may be as simple as a lender in California selling mortgage loans to another lender in New York, or as complex as the development and sale of Government National Mortgage Association (GNMA) pass-through securities, which are guaranteed by GNMA and are backed by a pool of mortgages worth millions of dollars.

The need for protection from title problems is more acute

Title insurance guarantees that you have true entitlement to your property.

when dealing with mortgages in the secondary market than what is normally encountered by a local lender. Knowing the local customer and the attorney rendering an opinion may be sufficient for a local lender to provide financing using one of their portfolio lending programs. However, a title opinion from a local attorney will not provide the assurance for a national lender who is unfamiliar with local risks and/or unwilling to take a chance.

In view of these considerations, it's easy to see why virtually every mortgage traded in the secondary market is covered by a loan policy. With financially sound corporate insurers standing behind the validity and enforceability of mortgage liens, the marketability of insured loans is greatly improved.

Mortgage Investments

Mortgage loans on all types of real property constitute the nation's largest single category of institutional investment. Loan policies have enhanced the remarkable growth in the availability of mortgage funds, which has brought an impressive stimulus to real estate investment from coast to coast.

This expansive viability has been characterized by two major developments – both directly linked to title insurance.

- Mortgage investment has become more secure.
- Mortgage money has become widely available throughout the country through the post-World War II development of a nationwide secondary mortgage market.

Safety of investment ranks at least equally with return realized where institutional investors are concerned. This fiduciary emphasis on security by the lending community means that the protection brought to real estate transactions by title insurance is vital if mortgage money is to remain widely available. Without the title company's assurance that the lender has a valid and enforceable lien, and that the borrower has a marketable title, real estate investment would be considered highly speculative, and would not enjoy its current high acceptance among lending institutions.

Most lenders also know that the familiar ALTA Loan Policy, developed based on their input and voluntarily used by ALTA member title insurers, is a nationally prominent means of protection, and adds even greater facility to trading within the secondary market.

Chapter 5

The Title Commitment

The title commitment details the parties involved, as well as the lists, requirements, and exceptions in order to close a property transaction. This document, drawn up before closing, reflects who currently owns the property, provides a legal description, and includes the parcel identification number or tax identification number of the property.

By issuing a title commitment, the title agency is committing to issuing a title policy to the buyer, provided that the requirements of the title commitment are satisfied prior to closing. For this reason, you should always request a copy, and review your title commitment prior to closing. As a title agent, I'm amazed at how few buyers request a copy of their title commitment. You should review the title commitment thoroughly, and if you don't know how to read it, I would suggest having your title company or real estate attorney review it and explain it to you thoroughly.

The information on the title commitment is the result of information that shows up on the title search. The title search explores public records to find out who owns the property, and searches the public records for all liens, judgments, and claims of liens, etc. You should always have your title company perform a title search. If you're getting title insurance, you will always receive this search as part of issuing the final policy. Regardless of whether you're the buyer or seller, you'll still be held responsible if there is a problem with the chain of title. Saving a little money on title insurance now could cost you thousands of dollars in the long run.

There is both a Schedule A and a Schedule B on the title commitment form, but let's focus our attention on Schedule B.

Schedule B-I – Requirements

Schedule B of the title commitment is subdivided into Schedule B-I and Schedule B-II. Schedule B-I shows requirements that are necessary in order to close and issue the title insurance policy. Schedule B-II shows exceptions – items that the title policy will not cover. Schedule B-I is the requirements page, which lists the documents that must be produced and/or signed, as well as any items that need to be satisfied prior to closing. This is required at the closing of a property transaction in order for the title to be transferred from the seller to the buyer. Schedule B-I also lists all liens, such as mortgages, property taxes, judgments, code enforcement liens, and more, which must be released and satisfied at, or prior to, closing.

Schedule B-II – Exceptions

Schedule B-II lists the exceptions. This is another important part of your title commitment, and should be reviewed very carefully by you if you are the buyer. The reason that Schedule B-II is so important is that everything not covered by your title policy is listed here. Or, expressed another way, everything that could be wrong with this property will be listed in the Schedule B-II. If you're not sure what something is, you should ask your title company to explain it to you. Remember that you're responsible for what you sign. If you don't understand something, it's imperative that you consult with someone who does understand it, so that they can explain it to you in a way that you can easily understand.

Most properties have exceptions listed on Schedule B-II of the title commitment. Having exceptions listed is not a problem, but you should make sure that you know what they are. Some properties even have use restrictions in this section specifying what you can and cannot do with your property.

Ultimately, it's the responsibility of the seller to cure these title defects and to deliver a clear and marketable title to the buyer. It is the responsibility of the buyer to read their title commitment and ask questions about all the requirements and exceptions prior to closing. Do not sign until you're convinced that all requirements have been satisfied. If you're unsure about anything, make sure that you consult with the title company.

Be especially cautious of title companies that work for the bank because they might be more interested in their relationship with the bank than their relationship with you. These title companies generally are not looking out for your best interests, and it's important for both consumers and real estate professionals to realize this and take it into consideration. The process and ease of closing on a property may depend on it.

Marked Up Title Commitment

A marked up title commitment is where Schedule B-I is marked satisfied, which indicates that all of the requirements have been cleared. The final markup of the title commitment indicates which items are covered and which are excluded, and is the best form of evidence of insurance from the title company.

In the eleven years that I've been in the title insurance business, this is one item that I find only experienced people ask for. But as a buyer, lender, investor, or real estate agent, you want to make sure that those requirements have been completed. You want to know to ask for this document, and you want to know how to go over it.

This is your written proof that the title company has satisfied these items properly in order to clear the title. Only experienced real estate professionals ask for a marked up title commitment, but you should always do so as well. Remember that you're responsible for what you sign, and you should seek clarification for anything you don't understand. Ask questions of the professionals, so you have a good idea about what's going on.

You should also make sure that the title company is working for you and not for someone else (like the seller, bank, real estate agent, or mortgage broker, etc.). This is one of the main reasons that we tell our customers/clients to choose their own title company. If you control where the closing takes place, you're able to guide the closing to your title company, who will look out for your best interests.

Title Policy

A title policy is the final document you receive post-closing, detailing what's covered and what's not covered in your title insurance policy.

A title insurance policy contains provisions for the payment of the legal fees in defense of a claim against your property, which is covered under your policy. It also contains provisions for indemnification against losses, which result from a covered claim. If you acquire a title insurance policy, you derive the knowledge that recorded matters have been searched and examined so that title insurance covering your property can be issued.

Remember that you're responsible for what you sign.

You receive this policy from the title company or real estate attorney after the closing of a real estate transaction. This document is usually in the same package as the original recorded deed.

If there were ever a problem with the title to the property, you would want to make sure that you had your title policy available so it's a good idea to save it, even after you've sold the property. If there's ever a problem with the chain of title on this property, you'll need to produce this title policy to prove that you were protected.

Another reason to save your title policy is that if you sell the property within three years from the date of purchase, or refinance at any time, you'll be eligible to receive a reissue credit, which will substantially reduce your title policy premium on the new transaction.

The Owner's Title Policy

Sometimes title problems occur over information that couldn't be found in the public records, or facts that are inadvertently missed in the title search process. To help protect you in these events, I recommend that you obtain an owner's policy of title insurance to insure you against the most unforeseen problems. Owner's title insurance, called an owner's policy, is usually issued in the amount of the real estate purchase. It's purchased for a one-time fee at closing, and lasts for as long as you or your heirs have an interest in the property. Only an owner's policy fully protects the buyer should a covered title problem arise with the title that wasn't found during the title search. Possible hidden title problems can include:

- Errors or omissions in deeds
- Mistakes in examining records
- Forgery
- Undisclosed heirs

An owner's policy provides assurance that your title company will stand behind you monetarily and with legal defense if needed, in case a covered title problem arises after you buy your home. The bottom line is that your title company will be there to help pay valid claims and cover the costs of defending an attack on your title. Receiving an owner's policy isn't always an automatic part of the closing process, and is paid for by different people in different parts of the country. Be sure you request an owner's policy and ask how it is paid for where you live. No matter who pays for the owner's policy, the fee is a one-time fee paid at closing.

The Loan Policy

During this process of attaining the title commitment, it's important that you exercise your rights for insurance and loans. There are two types of title insurance: owner's title insurance and lender's title insurance, also called a loan policy. Most lenders require a loan policy when they issue you a loan. The loan policy is based on the dollar amount of your new loan. It only protects the lender's interests in the property should a problem with the title arise. The policy amount decreases each year, and eventually disappears when the loan is paid off.

What is Owner's Title Insurance?

Title insurance is insurance, just like any other insurance, except that the owner's title insurance insures against defects in ownership. A policy of title insurance is like a pre-paid legal agreement: the title insurer will provide legal defense against challenges to the buyer's insured title (dependent, of course, upon the type of policy coverage), and will reimburse the buyer financially for losses due to covered defects in the buyer's ownership rights. An owner's policy assures buyers that the title to the real estate is free from all defects, liens, and encumbrances, except those listed as exceptions in the policy or excluded from the policy's coverage. It also covers losses and damages suffered if the title is unmarketable. The policy also provides coverage for loss if there is no right of access to the land.

An owner's title insurance comes highly recommended because of the protection it provides. If you ever have a lender tell you that an owner's policy is not necessary (so you can save some money), you ought to ask them why, then, they require you to pay for a lender's policy to protect them. If you ever have a real estate agent tell you an owner's policy is unnecessary you ought to get that in writing as evidence of the bad advice, so you can later sue him or her.

So, you may be asking: Doesn't the lender's title insurance policy protect me? The answer is no. It is called a lender's policy because the lender is the insured, not the buyer, which means the buyer has no rights whatsoever under that policy. First, an owner is not compensated for the equity in the property. Second, even if the lender's policy "pays off" what in effect happens, the title insurance company will buy the note from the lender.

Many homebuyers are confused about the difference between a lender's policy and an owner's policy. A lender's title policy will only cover the amount that is at risk for the lender, which is generally not the actual full amount of the purchase price. Virtually every lender in the country requires title insurance for its mortgage loans to protect themselves.

An owner's title policy, on the other hand, is written specifically for the benefit of the owner. The small, additional expense of adding an owner's policy to the purchase made for the benefit of the lender is generally a bargain. The one-time premium covers the property for as long as the owner has an interest in the property. The coverage automatically continues for the benefit of the heirs in the event of a death.

Chapter 6

Title Terms, Roles, and Tasks

As a consumer, it's important that you understand the roles of the different people involved in title insurance. These individuals are the title underwriter and the title examiner.

Title Insurance Underwriter

The title insurance underwriter is the company that issues the title insurance policy. In Florida, the most common underwriters are Westcor Land Title Insurance Company, Old Republic National Title Insurance Company, First American Title Insurance Company and Stewart Title Guaranty Company. These companies issue title policies that cover any problems with the property, as long as the problem is not listed in Schedule B-II of the title commitment. (This is exactly why you should review the Schedule B-II so thoroughly before closing.)

Title Examiner

The title examiner is the individual that performs the title examination. Based on the results of title examination carried out by the examiner, the title commitment and title policy are issued by the title company. Any exceptions listed on Schedule B-II of the title commitment need to be reviewed and cleared by the examiner as they are completed. This will be done in the marked up title commitment. If there is a problem with the title, the title company will contact the examiner to have them review the issue and see if they can come up with a solution to resolve it. If they can, then the underwriter will "insure over" the issue, meaning that they are prepared to insure the transaction and issue a title policy without listing the item as an exception. Good title companies have good relationships with the title examiner and underwriter, so that any issues that come up can immediately be resolved.

Title Examination

Title examination is the process of researching the history of a specific property's title. The title examiner will research the history of the property and compile a title research report in a process known as a title examination. The title examination will trace the transfer of ownership (title) of the land going back to the first purchaser, and may research the history of the property for a period of thirty years. It is a relatively simple procedure to trace ownership of the property as it transferred from one owner to another. This chain of title shows the history of transfer of ownership of the property, and is what a title search is all about.

Many varied and complex issues may arise during a normal title examination. Researching the title to a property can get complicated because previous owners may have died, for instance, leaving title to the property to their heirs, as

You cannot afford not to have title insurance.

designated by a will or trust. Or, the owner of a property could have filed bankruptcy, in which case the title could have been transferred to the bankruptcy trustee. The title to the property could be in the name of a limited liability company, also known as an LLC, of which one of the partners may be involved in a lawsuit. There may be federal tax liens placed against an owner of the property, or one of the previous owners may have been in foreclosure.

You can buy a property without title insurance, but you would be foolish to do so. A thorough title examination, along with a title insurance policy, will insure that your title is well inspected and your investment is protected.

Property, Land, or Boundary Surveys

Professional surveys should also be completed on a property to ensure that it's in good order to be sold. If you are buying, selling, or planning to refinance or make improvements to your property, the lender and the building department will require that you have a boundary survey and an elevation certificate.

Did you know that having a boundary (land) survey and elevation certificate are considered improvements to the property? And, they are both for your benefit, as well as the buyer.

Boundary Survey

A boundary survey shows the boundary of your property, which is where your property ends and your neighbor's begins. The boundary survey provided by a professional surveyor and cartographer (map maker) graphically shows any possible encroachments or easement violations, which could prevent the owner from selling the land or making improvements to it. It is critical to know if there are concrete slabs, fences, or structures, including utilities, within easements or built onto the adjacent property.

Elevation Certificate

The elevation certificate shows how high the lot sits relative to the surrounding land. Elevation is important if you are in a flood zone, since properties that are elevated will have less risk of flooding, while properties that are not will have an increased risk.

A flood assessment determines if your property sits in a flood zone. The lender will require an elevation certificate if the property is located in a Federal Emergency Management Agency (FEMA) flood hazard zone, and will require you to purchase flood insurance to protect against the risk of flood. The elevation certificate shows how high above the pre-determined base flood elevation the structure sits, as well as the elevations adjacent to the building, and will determine how much premium you pay for your flood insurance policy.

Lenders will also require that you show proof of flood insurance prior to loaning against the property. The lender can offer you a flood insurance policy, but the premium will be very high since they'll assume the worst elevation. Purchasing an elevation certificate will enable you to get an accurate assessment and pay less for flood insurance, since the elevation certificate will indicate the relative risk of flooding to the insurance company. If you are located in a flood zone, purchasing an elevation certificate will save you a lot of money in insurance premiums over the long haul.

Now, let's talk more about some title problems that can arise when purchasing or selling a property.

Chapter 7

Common Title Problems

Of course even with the most careful research and processing, title problems are a possibility. There are a range of different possible problems, and a number of ways to protect yourself from them. The first step, of course, is education. Here are some stories on common title problems:

Fraud and Forgery

Those involved in real estate fraud and forgery can be clever and persistent, which can spell trouble for your home purchase. These people operate in a number of different ways, but understanding the most common routes to fraud can help you protect yourself.

In one example, an innocent buyer in a western state purchased an attractive home site through a realty company, accepting a notarized deed from the seller. Then another couple, the true owners of the property — who lived in another locale — suddenly appeared and initiated legal action to prove that their interest in the real estate was valid.

Under the owner's title insurance policy of the innocent buyer, bought for a one-time fee at closing, the title company provided a money settlement to protect against financial loss.

As it turned out, the forger spent time in advance at the local courthouse, searching the public records to locate property with out-of-town owners who had been in possession for an extended period. The individual then forged and recorded a deed to a fictitious person and assumed the identity of that person before listing the property for sale to an innocent purchaser, handling most contacts through an answering service. The identity of the notary appearing on deeds was fictitious as well. So this fraudulent person received money for the sale of a property that didn't actually belong to them.

Forgery is becoming big in today's real estate market. We had a closing that was supposed to take place with a son and mother selling a property. The son came to closing with a quit claim deed signed by his mother. This was giving the son full control of the property and the proceeds. There was an error on the deed in that it was missing a notary's signature. We notified the son that the deed needed to be re-signed.

He proceeded to leave the office and added a fake signature to the deed. He then got the deed recorded and brought it back. We knew this was not the case as the mother was in northern Florida and this was in southern Florida. It was later discovered that the son forged his mother's signature on the original deed. She was in a nursing home in northern Florida and had no clue this transaction was taking place. The son was hoping to be able to sell the property without his mother knowing and take all of the proceeds for himself.

Fraud and forgery are examples of hidden title hazards that can remain undetected until after a closing, despite the most careful precautions. Although emphasizing risk elimination, an owner's policy also protects you financially through negotiation by the insurer with third parties, payment for defending against an attack on the title as insured, and payment of valid claims.

Conflicting Wills

Conflicts over a will from a deceased former owner may suggest a study topic for law school. But the subject can take on real dimension, and all too quickly, when your home ownership is at stake.

In another example, after purchasing a residence, a new owner was startled when a brother of the seller claimed an ownership interest and sought a substantial amount of money as his share. It seemed that their late mother had given the house to the son making the challenge, who placed the deed in his drawer without recording it at the courthouse. Some twenty years later, after the death of the mother, the deed was discovered and then filed. Permission was granted in probate court to remove the property from the late mother's estate, and the brother to whom the residence was initially given sold the house.

However, the other brother appealed the probate court decision, claiming their mother really didn't intend to give the house to his sibling. Ultimately, the appeal was upheld and the new owner faced a significant financial loss. Since the new owner had acquired an owner's policy of title insurance upon purchasing the real estate, the title company paid the claim, along with an additional amount in legal fees incurred during the defense.

Missing Heirs

When buying a home, it's important to take into account that you might not be operating with all the facts. And if there's a missing heir in the situation, what you don't know may just kill your chances at purchasing the home.

Fraud and forgery are examples of hidden title hazards that can remain undetected until after a closing.

Here's an example: A couple purchased a residence from a widow and her daughter, the only known heirs of the husband and father who died without leaving a will. Soon after the sale, a man appeared, claiming he was the son of the late owner by a former marriage. As it turned out, he was indeed the son of the deceased man. This legal heir disapproved of his father's remarriage and had vanished when the wedding took place. Nonetheless, the son was entitled to a share of the value of the home, which meant an expensive problem for the unwary couple purchasing the property.

Although the absence of a will hindered discovery of the missing heir in a title search of the public records, an owner's policy of title insurance issued for a one-time fee at the time of the real estate transaction would have financially protected the couple from the claim by the missing heir.

An owner's policy is necessary to fully protect a homebuyer in any of these situations. Lender's title insurance, which is usually required by the mortgage lender, serves as protection only for the lending institution. So it's important that you maintain an owner's policy throughout, for your own protection. Never let anyone talk you out of this, as it can leave you open to the possibility of fraud or other title problems.

Chapter 8

Municipal and Government Lien Search

Another way to protect yourself from title problems is to make sure that a lien search is done on the property. A lien is meant to protect parties that have an interest in the property. A lien search discovers whether there are any unresolved and unrecorded liens against the property, such as unpaid utility bills. Searching the records for liens provides a basis for title insurance, and usually includes visits to the offices of recorders or registers of deeds, clerks of courts, and other officials.

In many jurisdictions, information about a piece of property and any liens against it is filed in different ways. This information can be filed under the seller's name, the owner's name, by lot number, or by street address. To make the search process less cumbersome, many title companies have created title plants, which contain virtually all the information from the county records, but indexed in a consistent matter (i.e., by name or lot number) so that title searches may be performed more quickly and accurately. In major metropolitan areas, the title can be searched and title insurance issued within twenty-four to forty-eight hours.

Never refrain from ordering a lien search when you're closing on a real estate

The following story about lien searches shows why it's a good idea to involve the title company in the early stages of a land transfer: In one transaction, the title search revealed that 2 acres of land being purchased were once part of a 5-acre tract. A prior deed to the

5 acres of land restricted use of the property to "a single family dwelling and the usual out-buildings." The other 3 acres from the original tract already contained a single family dwelling, and there was a serious question as to whether the purchaser could build a home on his 2 acres. With assistance from the title company, releases were obtained from the appropriate parties to remove the problem and allow the house to be built. Without that search, though, the purchaser would have run into legal problems down the line.

Occasionally, title problems may be so serious that the most prudent course is to end a transaction. For example, a buyer was about to close his purchase when the title search revealed pipeline, utility, flood, and road easements across the property, which would have severely limited his use of the land. When these findings became known, the buyer declined to continue with the transaction. Only a title search would have uncovered these problems.

In Florida, a lien search is sometimes called a Chapter 159 search, based on Florida Statute Chapter 159. A lien search is also sometimes referred to as a municipal lien search or unrecorded lien search. Lien searches can be required for the purposes of issuing title insurance to a lender and/or purchaser. Although the term lien search is not commonly used nationwide, the function of gathering pertinent information prior to closing remains unchanged. This is typically the responsibility of the settlement agent. A lien search for unrecorded property debt can also be conducted by any party interested in conducting due diligence on a particular property.

Interested parties, such as title companies, banks, mortgage companies, and individuals, can request that the city check its records for outstanding liens, fines, and fees against a property. For a fee, the city will search its records and report any liens that appear in the records, as well as any other known outstanding charges or assessments against the property. The accrued interest charges on the liens, as well as the lien fees that must be paid in order to have the liens removed from the public records of the specific county with which they are recorded, will also be reported on the lien search report from the city. Lien searches are usually completed within five to seven business days of receiving the formal request and payment.

Different Types of Liens

Various types of municipal and government liens can show up in a lien search. When various fines, fees, or charges remain unpaid by a property owner, the city can exercise its legal right to place a lien against an owner's property to ensure the eventual collection of an unpaid amount. These liens may be for:

- Water and Utility Bills (an electric bill is not a lien)
- Unpaid Property Taxes
- Notice of Commencement and Mechanic Liens
- Open Permits
- Unsafe Structure/Demolition and Securing Liens
- Property Maintenance Liens
- Code Enforcement Liens
- Code Enforcement Violations
- Judgments Against all Owners
- IRS and Federal Tax Liens

Please remember that the above liens may not show up in a title search. However, they may show up in a lien search. For this reason you should never refrain from ordering a lien search when you're closing on a real estate transaction.

Whose Responsibility is it To Get a Release of Lien?

You can stipulate in the agreement with your contractor that he must provide all releases of lien. If it's not a part of the contract, however, or you act as your own contractor, then YOU must get the releases. If you borrow money to pay for the improvements and the lender pays the contractor(s) directly without obtaining releases, the lending institution may be responsible to you for any loss.

If you don't get releases of liens, you will not be able to sell your property unless all outstanding liens are paid. Sometimes a landowner can even be forced to sell their property to satisfy a lien. In addition, contractors, laborers, materials suppliers, subcontractors, and professionals such as architects, landscape architects, interior designers, engineers, and land surveyors all have the right to file a claim of lien for work or materials. Always require a release of lien from anyone who does work on your property.

Contesting a Lien

A lien is valid for one year, unless a lien holder files a lawsuit to enforce the lien prior to the expiration of the year. An owner has a right to file a notice of contest of lien during the one-year period. Upon the filing of a notice of contest of lien, the lien holder must file a lawsuit to enforce the lien within sixty days. Failure of the lien holder to file a timely lawsuit renders the lien invalid.

Judgments Against all Owners

In a civil court case, after a judge or jury hands down a verdict, or after a court-approved settlement, a judgment is entered by the court. As part of a typical judgment, the court orders the payment of money from one person to another. But the person who owes the money (the debtor) doesn't always pay up. A judgment lien is one way to ensure that the person who won the judgment (the creditor) gets what he or she is owed. A judgment lien gives the creditor the right to be paid a certain amount of money from proceeds from the sale of the debtor's property.

In Florida, a judgment lien can be attached to the debtor's real estate, meaning a house, condo, land, or similar kind of property interest. Florida also allows judgment liens to be attached to the debtor's personal property – things like jewelry, art, antiques, and other valuables. This judgment lien can remain attached to the debtor's property (even if the property changes hands) for ten years (real estate lien) or five years (personal property lien). Keep in mind that in Florida, a creditor's ability to collect under a judgment lien will be affected by several factors, including a fixed amount that is untouchable if the property is the debtor's primary residence (called a homestead), other liens that may be in place, and any foreclosure or bankruptcy proceedings.

Where Can I Look up Florida Law on Judgment Liens?

If you want to go right to the source and look up Florida laws on judgment liens or maybe you're a party to a judgment, or you're just researching potential encumbrances on property – the relevant statute(s) can be found at Fla. Stat. Ann. Sections 55.202 to .205, 55.081, and 55.10.

Chapter 9

Department of Housing and Urban Development (HUD)

The Department of Housing and Urban Development (HUD) is a cabinet department in the Executive branch of the United States federal government. Although its beginnings were in the House and Home Financing Agency, it was founded as a Cabinet department in 1965, as part of the "Great Society" program of President Lyndon Johnson, to develop and execute policies on housing and metropolises.

According to their official website, *"HUD's mission is to create strong, sustainable, inclusive communities and quality affordable homes for all. HUD is working to strengthen the housing market to bolster the economy and protect consumers; meet the need for quality affordable rental homes: utilize housing as a platform for improving quality of life; build inclusive and sustainable communities free from discrimination; and transform the way HUD does business."*

A HUD-1 settlement statement is basically a document prepared by a closing agent describing a real estate transaction, including the escrow deposits for taxes, commissions, loan fees, points, hazard insurance, and mortgage insurance. It's also called a closing statement or settlement sheet.

The HUD issues a settlement statement prior to closing, known as a HUD-1, for each and every property transaction. This is your final account of all of the costs and figures related to the closing transaction (closing costs). Many of the costs listed in the HUD-1 form should also have been included in the Good Faith Estimate (GFE) of mortgage costs, which you should have received from your lender. However, the HUD-1 amounts are final and the Good Faith Estimate is not. For this reason, you should always review the HUD before you get to the closing table.

How to Read Your HUD-1

We will now take a closer look at the different sections of the HUD-1 form. In each section, there is one column showing the buyer's (or borrower's) figures and another column showing the seller's figures. Use these to learn the process.

- **Sections A through I – General Information**: The form starts with basic information about your loan. This includes such information as the type of loan, loan number, closing agent file number, location of the closing, and the settlement date or date of closing. It also contains the buyer, seller, and/or borrower's information, as well as the property address.
- **Section B – Type of Transaction:** There are several types of transactions. Examples include Cash Purchase, FHA, Conventional Uninsured, VA, or Conventional Insured.
- **Section B – File Number:** This is the settlement agents file number.
- **Section B – Loan Number:** This is the lender's loan number.
- **Section B – Mortgage Insurance Case Number:** This is the mortgage insurance case number assigned to the closing.

- **Section C – Note:** Disclosure.
- **Section D:** Name and address of the buyer/borrower.
- **Section E:** Name and address of the seller.
- **Section F:** Name and address of the lender.
- **Section G:** Property address.
- **Section H:** Settlement agent and location of the closing.
- **Section I:** Settlement Date or Closing Date.
- **Section J - Summary of Buyers/Borrower's Transaction:** Section J shows the gross totals of the buyer's costs and credits, and the net amount the buyer will owe for the purchase. The total is listed by category:
  - **100 – Gross Amount Due From Borrower**: This is the amount the buyer owes, consisting of the property purchase price, the fees or settlement charges, items such as appliances purchased from the seller, and payment of taxes the seller has prepaid (Line 120 is the total).
  - **200 – Amounts Paid by or on Behalf of Borrower**: These are the amounts the buyer has paid, such as the deposit, or financed, such as the mortgage financing or a mortgage the buyer is assuming. It also includes any sums the seller owes the buyer, such as unpaid taxes, utility costs, or allowances for repairs (Line 220 is the total).
  - **300 - Cash at Settlement From/To Borrower**: This carries the totals down to the bottom of the page. Line 301 is the same as Line 120. Line 302 is the same as Line 220. Line 303 is the total cash to/from the buyer at closing.
- **Section K – Summary of Seller's Transaction:** Section K shows the gross total of the seller's costs and credits, and the net amount the seller will owe or receive for the sale. It lists the totals by category:

- **400 – Gross Amount Due to Seller**: This reflects the credits due to the seller at closing, like the sales price of the home and/or any personal property that is being purchased by the buyers (Line 420 is the total).
- **500 – Reductions in Amount Due to Seller**: This reflects the charges or the debits of the seller. Examples include the settlement charges paid by the seller (Line 502), payoffs of existing loans, and proration's of items such as taxes and assessments to be credited to the buyer at closing (line 520 is the total).
- **600 – Cash at Settlement From/To Seller**: This carries the totals down to the bottom of the form. Line 601 is the same as line 420. Line 602 is the same as line 520. Line 603 is the cash due to/from Seller at closing.

- **Section L (Settlement Charges):** Section L, on the second page of the form, shows all the specific costs for financing and processing of the transaction. It includes:
  - **700 – Total Sales/Broker's Commission based on sales price**: This is the commission charged by the real estate broker.
  - **800 – Items Payable In Connection with the Loan**: This includes the loan origination fee, any discount points paid to reduce the mortgage rate, the appraisal fee and credit report fee, the application fee for mortgage insurance, and the assumption fee, if you've assumed an existing mortgage. Fees that have been paid up front are marked POC (paid outside of closing) and will not be included in the total on Line 1400.
  - **900 – Items Required by Lender to be Paid in Advance**: This is the interest on the loan for the period before the first monthly payment, and the

initial mortgage insurance and hazard or home insurance premiums (often covering the first year).

- **1000 – Reserves Deposited With Lender**: These are escrow items, which the lender holds to cover future expenses like property taxes and annual assessments. In some cases, you may be asked to remit future hazard and mortgage premiums as escrow items. There is a maximum that can be charged.

- **1100 – Title Charges**: These are the costs of changing ownership of the property, such as the title services and cost of title insurance. If the fee is payable to a third party, such as the notary or attorney, it is indicated. If one agent performs more than one service, the fees may be lumped together on one line.

- **1200 – Government Recording and Transfer Charges**: City, county, and state taxes or stamps needed to transfer ownership are listed here. The buyer often pays the deed and mortgage recording fees.

- **1300 – Additional Settlement Charges**: These include items such as surveys, inspections for such things as pests and lead-based paint, and home warranties.

- **1400 – Total Settlement Charges**: This is the sum total of all of the above fees. The amount listed in the buyer's (or borrower's) column should be identical to the amount listed as "settlement charges to borrower" on page 1, line 103, while the amount in the seller's column should be the same as the "settlement charges to seller" on page 1, line 502.

Harmful Fees That Could Appear on the HUD-1

Consumers should be aware of a relatively new legal instrument, called Wall Street Home Resale Fees (also known as private transfer fees). While traditional covenants have an accepted and beneficial role in the housing market by benefitting the land, these for-profit covenants require homeowners to pay a premium for the right to sell their property.

These fees are typically placed on properties by developers, and often go unnoticed by unsuspecting homebuyers. Wall Street Home Resale Fees are inserted into home sale contracts by private third parties, and require that every time a home is sold for the next ninety-nine years, a percentage of the sale of the home (usually 1 percent) will be paid to the third party. In return, homeowners receive nothing but reduced home equity and a harder time selling their home. In contrast resale fees levied by homeowners' and condo associations' direct money back toward homeowners in the form of infrastructure and amenity improvements. This is what differentiates them from the private, for-profit transfer fee.

The American Land Title Association (ALTA) cautions consumers about the impact Wall Street Home Resale Fees have on real estate. When purchasing a home, read through your sales contract to make sure this fee is not attached to your house. If you believe a Wall Street Home Resale Fee has been placed on your property, send an email to ALTA.

It's important to read through the HUD-1 form carefully and make sure that it's complete and accurate. You and the settlement agent will then both sign it to authorize payment of the funds. Once that's done, the home is yours.

Chapter 10

Types of Deeds

Once you've signed all of the papers and you've purchased your property, the ownership of that property goes directly to you in the form of a deed. A deed is the document that transfers ownership of real estate. It contains the names of the old and new owners, a legal description or land description, and the parcel identification number of the property, and is signed by the person transferring the property. Below, is a list of various types of deeds.

Types of Deeds

Quit Claim Deed

A Quit Claim deed transfers the ownership interest the person has in the property. It's important to understand that if the person signing the Quit Claim has no ownership interest in the property, then the Quit Claim deed is worthless. I can quit claim the Brooklyn Bridge to you. However, since I don't have any ownership in the Brooklyn Bridge, the Quit Claim deed is worthless. For this reason, you should never transfer property with a Quit Claim unless it's an intra-family transfer and you know the owner. Quit claim deeds are often used in the case of divorce or transfer of a property between siblings or from parents to their children.

Warranty Deed

A warranty deed transfers your ownership interest in the property and explicitly promises and guarantees, to the buyer, that you have good and clear marketable title to the property. A warranty

77

deed may also promise to cure certain defects. This is the most common type of deed in the State of Florida.

The fine print in the title policy, like most title policies, states that,

> *"The coverage shall continue in force in favor of an insured only so long as the insured retains an estate or interest in the land ... or only so long as the insured shall have liability by reason of covenants of warranty made by the insured in any transfer or conveyance of the estate or interest."*

Grant Deed

A grant deed transfers your ownership interest and makes certain guarantees that the title hasn't already been transferred to someone else or been encumbered, except as described in the grant deed. Most states use a grant deed, which is substantially better than a Quit Claim deed.

Special Warranty Deed

A special warranty deed is the most common method that a bank uses to transfer title to a bank-owned property, and is also known as an REO (real estate owned). The special warranty deed is a deed in which the seller conveys title to the buyer and agrees to protect the buyer against title defects or claims asserted by the bank or any other people who feel that they have a right to assert a claim against the property. With a special warranty deed, the seller guarantees to the buyer that they have not done anything during the time that they held title to the property to impair the title in any way. For purposes of purchasing bank-owned properties, a special warranty deed is usually fine and customary.

A deed should always be signed, in front of a notary public, by the person who is transferring or selling the property. All title companies have notaries in order to facilitate this process. The notarization means that a notary public has verified that the signature on the deed is a real signature. The signature must be notarized before the deed can be recorded.

In the state of Florida, executed deeds need to contain a notary signature and two witnesses per signature. One of the witnesses can be the notary, but they must sign in both spots. If there are two parties signing the deed, and they're both in the same place at the same time, then the witness may sign for both parties. In the case of two parties that are signing at two different times and two different locations (not together), there will need to be four signature lines for the witnesses and two notary signatures. Remember that if you didn't witness the signature, you shouldn't be signing the documents.

Chapter 11

Florida Mortgages versus Deed of Trust

Florida housing lenders employ mortgages and deeds of trust for property sales. However, the state of Florida does not require a deed of trust by law at the time of sale of property. It's important that consumers know the difference, and understand how to follow along with this process.

Mortgage

The standard method of home financing employs a mortgage, which legally creates a lien against a property. The finance company holds the lien until the buyer meets all financial obligations. The mortgage is a document that contains the terms of the finance agreement, including the amount owed and the payment terms. Upon payment in full the lender will sign and record a satisfaction of mortgage in the county public records.

Deed of Trust

While the state of Florida does not require deeds of trust, the option can still be used when the goal is to provide additional protection for the finance company. A legal document is employed to create a holding entity for the ownership of the property, naming the finance company as beneficiary and a third party as trustee, who will deliver ownership of the property to the finance company in the case of loan default.

A trust deed is also known as a deed of trust, and is not the same as other types of deeds. A trust deed is not used to transfer property, but is really another term for a mortgage in states that are deed of trust states (see list below). Georgia calls their trust deed a security deed. Connecticut calls theirs a mortgage deed.

A trust deed transfers the title to a "trustee," which is often a trust or a title company, which then holds the land as security for a loan. When the loan is paid off, title is transferred to the borrower. It works very much the same as the way car companies hold the title to a vehicle until you have paid off your note on the car. The trustee has no powers to convey or transfer the property unless the borrower defaults on the loan. If the borrower defaults, then the trustee can sell the property and pay the lender back from the proceeds, without first going to court. This occurs only in states where a deed of trust is used.

The title remains in trust until the loan is paid.

Florida uses a mortgage and not a deed of trust, so you actually own the title to your property in Florida from the date of purchase with a lien secured for the mortgage financing.

Lien Theory

Florida is a "lien theory" state, where buyers keep the title to the property and the finance companies hold a lien against the property until all financial obligations are met.

The basic difference between the mortgage as a security instrument and a deed of trust is that in a deed of trust situation there are three parties involved – the borrower, the lender, and a trustee, whereas in a mortgage document there are only two parties involved – the borrower and the lender. In a deed of trust, the borrower conveys title to a trustee, who holds title to the property for the benefit of the lender. The title remains in trust until the loan is paid.

Often a title company, escrow company, or bank is listed as the trustee on the deed of trust. When the loan has been paid, the trustee will issue a release deed or trustee's deed of reconveyance.

82

This deed of reconveyance should be recorded at the county recorder's office, to make public notice that the loan has been paid and that the lender's interest in the property has ended.

Another difference between a mortgage and a deed of trust is the manner in which foreclosure proceedings take place. State law will determine the method of foreclosure to be used. Generally, the rules when using a deed of trust allow for a faster foreclosure time than with the judicial foreclosure required with a mortgage. Under a deed of trust, when the borrower defaults on the loan, the lender delivers the deed of trust to the trustee, who then is instructed to sell the property. After proper notices have been posted and rules are followed, the property is sold at a trustee's sale and the loan is paid.

Mortgages

So, let's delve deeper into the world of mortgages. A mortgage lender usually requires title insurance to protect the lender against loss resulting from claims by others against the mortgaged property. Thus, it requires a borrower to purchase a lender's policy when taking a mortgage loan. The coverage afforded under a lender's policy is usually based on the dollar amount of the loan, and protects the lender's interests in the property should a problem with the title arise. The coverage amount decreases each year and eventually disappears as the loan is paid off. RESPA prohibits home sellers from requiring home purchasers to purchase title insurance from a particular company. The premium for the lender's policy will be listed on the HUD-1.

Refinancing a Mortgage with Title Insurance

When a person refinances a mortgage loan, he or she obtains a new loan, even if the refinancing is through the original lender. Thus, when refinancing, a lender will again require a lender's title insurance policy to protect its investment in the property. However, a person will not need to purchase a new owner's title insurance policy because the one bought at the original closing remains in effect for as long as the person (or an heir) has an interest in the property.

If you want to save money on one of the most costly items connected with a home mortgage, learn these two words: **Reissue Rate**.

Reissue rates are discounts off the standard premiums charged on title insurance policies. Though the discounts vary from state to state and from title insurer to title insurer, according to industry standards these discounts average 50 to 60 percent. Reissue rates are normally available only on refinancing, but in some areas they can be obtained on home re-sales where a title search was performed relatively recently for the seller.

Here's how it works. Say you bought your home five years ago. Now you see mortgage interest rates in the mid-6% range and decide to refinance. Should you pay full price for another insurance policy? Given the fact that a comprehensive search of the public records on your property was performed just five years ago, there's no reason to have to pay for another full search.

That's why the title industry offers special discount pricing for instances such as refinancing. Rather than paying $1,200 for a new title policy, for example, why not take advantage of a reissue rate at $500 or $600?

Title insurers' policies sometimes severely restrict the eligibility period for obtaining reissue discounts. Others have strict rules requiring presentation of the prior title policy to the title agent, to prove that insurance still covers the dwelling. The rules and discounts are also regulated by state laws, so consumers need to ask what rules apply to their specific situation. Compare reissue title rates if you're shopping. Reissue rates may vary from title company to title company.

CHAPTER 12

Your Title Company or the Bank's Title Company?

In Florida, it's customary for the seller to pay for the title policy and pick the title agent. The exceptions are Broward and Miami-Dade Counties, where it's customary for the buyer to pay for the title policy and to pick the title agent. In Palm Beach County and the rest of Florida, it's customary for the seller to pay for the title policy. Usually whoever picks the title agent also pays for the title policy.

If you're buying bank-owned properties, you should be especially cautious. As I said earlier, if you're using the bank's title company, this means that the title company has a relationship with the seller (bank) and not with you. There have been several cases where our investors have used the bank's title company and had serious title defects and issues.

You don't want to let the bank choose your title company.

The title companies that represent the bank are typically known as "title mills," which means that they are closing hundreds of transactions per month for a single bank. This means that the bank is effectively the title company's biggest and best client, and so the title company is much more concerned about the relationship with the bank than with you. Another issue is that because they are processing so many files, they make many mistakes, which your title company, that represents you, may not make.

One example of an issue that we've seen is where there was open code enforcement violations secured against a property that was going to cost a buyer over $5,000 to remedy. It was the bank's title company's procedure to have the buyer sign a "hold harmless agreement," which effectively meant that the bank's title company was willing to close the transaction with a title defect and make it the buyer's problem. This is a classic example of why you don't want to let the bank choose the title company, even if it saves you money. You're better off paying for your own title policy and choosing your own title company such as Independence Title, which will have your best interests at heart.

Another example is where we have called for a re-foreclosure on a property due to an invalid legal description or not serving all parties notice of foreclosure. It was the position of the banks title company to insure against the problem, hoping to move the property off the banks book. If an issue arises later down the line, they will deal with it then.

The problem here is many people buying bank owned properties are going to fix them up and re-sell them to a buyer that will live in the property. This investor that will be fixing up the property will have a big problem trying to sell a few months later because of the sloppy work from the bank's title company. Yet another example of why you should always choose your own title company.

Title Company versus Attorney

One of the most common questions that I am asked is whether to use a title company or an attorney for the closing. There are advantages to both, and obviously I would prefer that you do your closing with us at Independence Title. However, in the interest of education, this chapter will go over the pros and cons of each.

Attorneys know the law much more than a title company would. For that reason, they usually charge more money. A closing at a law firm will typically cost quite a bit more than a closing at a title company. Since attorneys bill by the hour, their time is very valuable, and using their time will cost you for your closing. However, there could be some benefits, if, for example the attorney is your attorney and you are utilizing the attorney's other services (i.e., preparing a mortgage).

The disadvantage of using an attorney for your closing is that attorneys are not monitored as closely by the state. The Florida Bar already monitors attorneys, and presumably the attorney knows the law of what he/she can and cannot do in regard to escrow accounts, etc. However the state doesn't monitor them in regard to real estate transactions.

Title companies, on the other hand, have much stricter requirements with their underwriters. Typically an underwriter will require monthly reconciliation from a title company to verify escrow deposits and accounts, whereas attorneys do not necessarily have this requirement. Some measures have been put into place to monitor attorney escrow accounts more closely since recent fraud issues have been more common in the industry.

It's hard to generalize, but attorneys are, for the most part, more expensive. Some attorneys work for the banks and REO companies, and for this reason there may be a conflicts of interest. You should always have someone reviewing your title commitment and lien search who is not affiliated with the seller or working on behalf of the seller.

Most real estate companies in Florida have a financial connection to a title company. They suggest or encourage their agents to refer their clients to a specific title company for the simple fact that the real estate company makes an additional fee from the settlement on the property.

This is a lesson that you should always be careful when choosing your title company. Ask the title company first if they have any affiliations with the real estate agent, mortgage broker, lender, or seller in order to ensure that there is no conflict of interest.

Chapter 13

Title Companies and Escrow

When you're closing on a property, you need to think about how the title company or attorney will handle the escrow process. Escrow and title insurance perform vital functions in most exchanges of, or loans against real property. Escrows and title insurance are infrequently employed in personal property transactions.

What is Escrow?

An escrow is an arrangement in which a disinterested third party, called an escrow holder, holds legal documents and funds on behalf of a buyer, seller, and/or lender and distributes them according to the buyer's, seller's, and/or lender's instructions. It is very important they follow the specific directions as not doing so can cause the transaction to be reversed.

There are two important reasons for selecting an established, independent escrow firm or title insurance company. One is that real estate transactions require a tremendous amount of technical experience and knowledge to handle the process smoothly. The other is that the escrow holder will be responsible for safeguarding documents and properly distributing the purchase price.

The escrow process was developed to help facilitate the sale, purchase, or refinance of your home. Escrow services provided by an independent third-party should include:

- Acting as the impartial depository of documents and funds
- Processing and coordinating the flow of documents and funds
- Keeping all parties informed of the escrow progress
- Responding to the lender's requirements
- Securing the needed title insurance policy
- Obtaining approval of reports, inspections, and documents
- Prorating insurance, taxes, rents, etc.
- Income tax reporting for the gross proceeds of the transaction
- Recording the deed, loan documents, and all other documents necessary for insuring the transaction
- Working closely with 1031 tax deferred Exchange Company to complete transactions within IRS guidelines

It's generally difficult and often impossible for each party to a real property purchase or loan transaction (e.g., buyer, seller, lender, holder of an existing deed of trust) to meet and perform its transaction obligations simultaneously. Accordingly, the parties will generally employ an escrow – an independent party – to assure that each party to a transaction receives what it has been promised. The escrow may be a department of a title company (common in Northern California), a separate commercial entity (common in Southern California), a lawyer, or any other person or entity the parties choose.

Consider the following examples of the use of escrow and title insurance. A seller owns their real property residence free and clear of any liens. After the purchase and sale contract is signed, one of the agents (usually the agent of the seller) will open an escrow. Each party to the escrow (e.g., the seller, the buyer, and the lender) will submit escrow instructions to the escrow, describing that party's requirements for how the transaction is to proceed.

For example, the instructions will require the seller to execute and deliver to the escrow a deed to the property, and instruct the escrow to deliver that deed to the buyer when the escrow can deliver the purchase price to the seller (less title insurance premium and other closing costs that the seller has agreed to pay). The instructions will require the buyer to deliver their down payment to escrow, and instruct the escrow to deliver that money to the seller when the escrow is ready and they are able both to record the deed in the buyer's favor and to deliver to the buyer a policy of title insurance insuring the buyer's title to the property against unknown and undisclosed liens. The buyer's lender will "fund" the escrow with loan proceeds when the escrow is able to record both a deed executed by the seller in the buyer's favor and a deed of trust executed by the buyer in favor of the lender, and when the escrow is able to deliver to the lender a policy of title insurance insuring the buyer's clear title to the property.

If the seller owns the residence subject to two deeds of trust, the buyer most likely will be unwilling to purchase the property until these encumbrances are removed. Therefore, the lenders of the money secured by these existing deeds of trust will submit deeds of re-conveyance to the escrow, with instructions that the escrow may record these deeds of re-conveyance (thus extinguishing the liens) when the escrow is holding money for their account to pay the balance due on their notes. The seller will receive from escrow the purchase price, less closing costs and amounts paid to the holders of these prior deeds of trust.

Why Do I Need an Escrow?

Whether you are the buyer, seller, lender, or borrower, you want the assurance that no funds or property will change hands until ALL of the instructions in the transaction have been followed. The escrow holder has the obligation to safeguard the funds and/or documents while they are in their possession, and to disburse funds and/or convey title only when all provisions of the escrow have been complied with.

The principals to the escrow – buyer, seller, lender, and borrower – cause escrow instructions, most usually in writing, to be created, signed, and delivered to the escrow officer. If a broker is involved, he or she will normally provide the escrow officer with the information necessary for the preparation of your escrow instructions and documents.

The escrow officer will process the escrow, in accordance with the escrow instructions, and when all conditions required in the escrow can be met, the escrow will be "closed." Each escrow, although following a similar pattern, will be different in some respects, as it deals with YOUR property and the transaction at hand.

Who Chooses the Escrow?

The selection of the escrow holder is normally done by agreement between the principals. If a real estate broker is involved in the transaction, the broker may recommend an escrow holder. However, it is the right of the principals to use an escrow holder who is competent and who is experienced in handling the type of escrow at hand. Remember, only independent escrow corporations are licensed by the DOC. There are laws that prohibit the payment of referral fees; this affords the consumer the best possible escrow services without any compromise caused by a person receiving a referral fee.

What Do I Have to Do While in Escrow?

The key to a transaction as important as the sale, or purchase of your home, is to **read and understand** your escrow instructions. If you do not understand them, you should ask your escrow officer to explain the instructions, and consult your lawyer for legal advice. Do not expect your escrow officer to advise you as to whether or not you have a "good deal" or are doing things the right way. The escrow officer is there to follow the instructions given by the principals in the escrow.

If you're required to deliver funds into the escrow, make sure that you provide good funds in the form required by the escrow office. Escrow can only close on cleared funds, and the processing of a personal check can take days, possibly even a week or more.

What is a Closing Statement?

A closing statement, as discussed earlier, is an accounting, in writing, prepared at the close of escrow that sets forth the charges and credits of your account. The items shown on the statement will reflect the purchase price, the funds deposited or credited to your account, payoffs on existing encumbrances and/or liens, the costs for all services, and determination of the funds you are entitled to at the close of escrow. When you receive your closing papers, review the closing statement; it comes itemized, and reflects the financial aspects of your transaction. If anything does not make sense to you, you should ask your escrow officer for an explanation.

Your closing statement and all other escrow papers should be kept indefinitely for income tax purposes. Your accountant will need the information about the sale or purchase of the property, and the IRS or other agency may require you to prove your costs and/or profit on the sale of any property. The closing statement will assist in this task.

What Fees and Costs Will Be Charged?

Escrow fees are not regulated by the state. Escrow holders, like any other businesses, will charge fees that are commensurate with the costs of producing the service, the liability undertaken, and the overhead expenses which include a profit factor. Therefore, the fees will vary between companies and from county to county. Normally, the escrow holder will follow its minimum fee schedule, which will provide for extra charges based upon the differing elements of your escrow. On occasion, an additional fee will charged for unusual expenditures of time on a given transaction.

The escrow holder has no control over the costs of other services that are obtained, such as the title insurance policy, the lender's charges, hazard insurance, recording charges, etc. Your escrow officer, upon request, can provide you with an estimate of the escrow fees and costs, as well as fees charged by others, provided such information is available.

What about Cancellations?

No escrow is opened with the intention that it will be cancelled, but there are occasions when a contingency cannot be met, or when the parties disagree during the period that escrow is open. Some escrow holders provide for such an event by incorporating an instruction in the typed or printed general provisions.

Ordinarily, and escrow holder will take the position that no funds on deposit can be refunded until the escrow holder is in receipt of mutual cancellation instructions signed by the principals. The escrow holder cannot normally make a determination as to who is the "rightful" party in a dispute on a cancellation until the principals agree; the escrow holder is not a judge.

You can expect to be charged a cancellation fee, as this is a charge for professional services rendered, and quite often for several "out of pocket" expenses that have been incurred on the client's behalf. These fees can vary from company to company, depending upon their policies.

Sometimes, when a dispute exists, the escrow holder may be forced to allow a court to decide which party is entitled to what documents or funds; this is called an interpleader action. Fortunately, most disputes are resolved before the interpleader is filed, as the costs for such legal actions are extreme. Those costs, incidentally, are normally paid out of the funds on deposit in the escrow.

What about Property Taxes?

The terms of your transaction and the resultant escrow instructions determine how the property taxes will be handled. If there is no mention of the proration of taxes, your escrow officer will not deal with any credit or charges for prorated taxes; there will be an item in your closing statement that will reflect either a credit or charge to your account. If the taxes are not yet paid (even though there has been a credit or charge against your account), the buyer is obligated to obtain a tax bill and pay the taxes. If the buyer does not have a tax bill with which to pay the taxes, you can request a bill from the tax collector; send a photocopy of the deed.

Supplemental property tax is another concern of the buyer. Upon transfer of real property, the county assessor will request information to assist them in determining the value of the property for taxation purposes. Some of the information may have been previously supplied by the escrow holder at the time of the closing of the escrow, via preliminary change of ownership form that should accompany each deed when it recorded.

Does the Perfect Escrow Exist?

Perfection is sometimes difficult to achieve, especially in dealing with the complexities of the escrow, the desires of the parties, and other matters that are sometimes far beyond the control of the escrow officer. It is human nature to make a mistake on occasion, but if you have chosen an independent licensed escrow company, your escrow officer has the background, training, education, support, and systems in place necessary in order to accomplish the objectives of the escrow instructions.

In the event you have any problems in the handling of your escrow, you should first contact the escrow officer. If your problem is not resolved, you should next contact the management or owner of the company. If the matter requires additional attention, you can call the proper regulatory agency.

Escrow Agents

The escrow agent works for both the lender and the buyer, and their purpose is to carry out the instructions that both parties have agreed on. This person will release your money once all of the terms of your agreement have been upheld.

Your mortgage lender will more than likely require you to open an escrow account to make sure there is enough money to cover your insurance and taxes. The way this works is that you will make an initial deposit to your escrow account, followed by monthly instalments. Most lenders will arrange to have this included in your monthly mortgage payments. When your taxes and insurance premiums come due, the escrow agent will release the funds to the appropriate party.

The reason behind having an escrow account is to protect the lender in the event that you default on your payments. The lender is then protected from external perils that could arise as a result of you not paying your taxes, or your insurance causing the lender to be left with no collateral.

An escrow account also helps the buyer because it allows you to spread your payments evenly over a twelve-month period. Just imagine if your yearly taxes were $3,000 and your yearly insurance was $1,400 – that would leave you owing $4,400 in one lump sum.

Your escrow amounts could change from year to year, due to the possible increase in your taxes and insurance. Therefore, your lender will review and adjust your escrow amounts annually, and you will be given a revised mortgage payment if your taxes or insurance go up. On the same token, however, if your taxes or insurance rates go down, you will be given a refund.

Sometimes an escrow requirement can be waived. Some buyers prefer to pay all of their taxes and insurance directly. Your lender may allow you to do this if your down payment is more than 20 percent, but they will more than likely raise your interest rate slightly to compensate. One thing to remember is that once you begin putting your funds into an escrow account, it can be difficult to cancel this process. Make sure that you fully understand what your options are before moving forward.

Chapter 14

Title Companies and Closing Agents

Mortgage lenders and title companies employ notaries or closing agents to close mortgages. These are professionals with whom you should become familiar, and roles that you should understand, in order to protect yourself from fraud.

What is a Closing Agent?

A closing agent is an individual or company that coordinates closing-related activities, such as conducting the closing, recording the closing documents and disbursing funds per the closing instructions. Some define it as an individual or company who handles the closing and the legal transfer of title and ownership from the seller to the buyer. Also known as the Settlement Agent.

Not wanting to lose out to a competitive buyer, many borrowers want to know how to make settlement go as smoothly, and quickly, as possible. The right choice of a settlement agent is one way in which you can speed up your closing.

Basically, the settlement agent is the person who coordinates all the paper-pushing that goes into a closing. Generally, the agent has some sort of connection to a title insurance company.

Closing agents aren't all alike. You may have heard that title insurance rates and closing fees can vary from company to company, but you may not be aware of the differences in service you will receive from one company to the next.

Many borrowers aren't aware that they have the right to choose title insurance agents. Under the federal Real Estate Settlement Procedures Act, the seller cannot require you to buy title insurance from a particular title company. The lender may request that you use a title company it finds acceptable, and it likely will recommend some companies, but in most cases you will have a choice. The lender will almost always agree with your pick.

Closing is about preparation and service. Expect good service, and ask for it. Making the right choice ahead of time will be the magic key that opens the door to a speedy settlement. Ask how quickly a title search can be performed. Ask the turnaround time for issuing a title commitment or title report. Ask who will communicate with the lender, appraiser, real estate agent, inspector, and lawyer, if one is involved. Some title officers or closing agents don't have assistants to help them get the reports out quickly. They can become bogged down with files, and yours may be on the bottom of the stack.

When selecting a title company or closing agent, ask ahead of time what kind of service you can expect.

Chapter 15

Title Insurance and Foreign Buyers

Everything about getting title insurance for the purchase or sale of real estate for people living in the US, also applies to those planning on moving to the US. Investing in Florida real estate comes with its list of challenges and complications, especially for overseas investors, but if you have all the correct information, investing is simple. Brokering such deals can be highly beneficial as a real estate professional, and if you approach the process in the correct way, you can easily sell some of the more expensive homes in your portfolio to overseas buyers. Most overseas buyers will be looking for a retirement home, but others will be looking to invest in a property for vacation rental or long-term rental purposes in order to gain regular income.

Florida is well established for overseas investors with the Florida Land Trust, which offers investors more flexibility and protection. There are also 1031 exchanges and other details in Florida Property Law, making the purchasing of property here fairly straight-forward. Lately, builders have also focused their attention on the domestic market and not so much on short-term vacation home rentals. This means that vacation homes will eventually become scarce, causing the existing homes to appreciate in value.

Many investors look to invest in Florida for a number of reasons. The cheap prices are what initially attract people, but they will also discover that Florida has the ideal climate with mild winters and pleasant summers, making it perfect for vacation homes or long-term rental homes. The vast number of tourist attractions also draws people to invest here.

According to the National Association of Realtors and the Florida Association of Realtors, about 25 percent of international property investors are from Canada, with 21 percent being from the United Kingdom and a further 21 percent coming from the rest of Europe. This can help you when setting up your marketing campaign, as it tells you exactly where to target your efforts.

Many people looking for bargains in the United States often look to Florida (one of the so-called Sand States) because of the severely depressed property market. They can have all the security, prestige, and profitability that come with a US property, but at very cheap prices, with the more distressed homes being snapped up ferociously by foreign investors. Many investors choose to rent the properties out to cover the mortgage until the market improves, and Canadians particularly enjoy purchasing near Florida's cruise ports to make the most of vacation rentals.

Processes Involved for a Foreign National

The first step in the process of investing in Florida real estate is to reserve a property for sale. This reservation amount is usually 20 percent to 30 percent of the market price of the property. The foreign investor will need to have a US bank account set up in order to facilitate the transaction, and may also need to provide six months' worth of bank statements showing their current loan repayments in order for the transaction to proceed.

Getting a mortgage in Florida is a straightforward process (although difficult to actually get), subject to a deposit being put down (usually it's a much larger deposit for foreign investors) and income verification processes, as well as a comprehensive and current valuation of the property by a professional appraiser. In the mortgage market, a foreign investor will be known as a Foreign National (or FN), and

It's the job of the title agency to make sure that the closing happens.

you will find FN Loans available from various asset lenders or private lenders, though it can be difficult to find people willing to finance a foreigner.

Other costs involved are closing costs on every real estate purchase, document stamp tax and the note stamp. Some new loans are also required to pay intangible tax. These costs, however, are minimal, and work out to about two percent of the purchase price of the property. Additionally, they are only incurred if the investor is using US financing to purchase the property. Therefore, an investor using money from outside the US for the purchase will experience reduced closing costs. On the other hand, money coming into the country via either cash or loan will be subject to other costs.

Possible Problems for Overseas Buyers

The main pitfalls to look out for when trying to sell investment property in Florida, or invest in the area, include:

- Financing can be tricky.
- Substantial down payments may be required.
- Mortgage insurance might be needed.
- Florida is a hurricane area, so comprehensive property insurance is vital, but can also be costly.
- For condo purchases, fees could be expensive depending on how much of the building is vacant or under foreclosure.
- Rental income taxation law will be in effect on both sides of the border, which can be costly.
- A managing agent in the area will need to be appointed to take care of the property, which can be part of the service Realtors offer their investors. This is not only practical, as there might be instances where access is required for workmen etc., but it is also a legal requirement. Property management is considered to be a job, and as a foreigner, there is no special work visa for this situation.

If you do have an overseas buyer interested in a Florida property, explaining this process to them will be highly beneficial.

- First, they should hire a property management agency (or your company if you offer this).
- Then, they should submit a W-8ECI form for tax filing purposes and obtain a Tax Identification Number (TIN).
- They must ensure that they have the funding in the US in order to proceed in the most effective and affordable way.
- They should then establish an LLC (Limited Liability Company) or Florida Land Trust (as discussed in a later chapter) to protect their asset.

International Funds

One of the most complex aspects of investing in Florida real estate, if you are a foreigner, is the international funding and taxations. If the foreign investor is transferring funds from outside of the US, there are certain implications that investors should understand.

First, the international funds might take a long time to clear and become available for use in property investing. A property fund can be created specifically for the purposes of investing, but can be risky in that the funds are unregulated.

If a foreign investor decides to bring cash money into the US amounting to more than $10,000, it must be reported to the federal government. They want to know everything about the money and how it was obtained, and thus they require the names of anyone connected with the cash, including brokers, agents, banks, attorneys, etc. A loan from overseas will also be determined as a cash transaction, because the loan is closed outside of the United States.

Approaching a lender inside the United States is an option, but not many lenders offer international loans, and those who do have very high interest rates. It is almost impossible for them to gauge a foreigner's credit payment history. Proof in the form of official letters or statements will need to be provided from previous lending institutions, stating that you have an excellent track record of making payments on time and when due.

Most experts suggest, however, that overseas investors acquire a loan in their country or origin, after which they should transfer and "season" the money in their US bank account for a period of time – usually two to three months, though it can be as long as six months, as mentioned previously.

International Currency Exchange

The currency exchange rate is something that foreign investors will have to keep in mind when purchasing and selling property. The exchange rate could change in their favor or against it, without warning, but the initial choice of where to get a mortgage will be determined by the currency exchange. Some banks have a stricter policy regarding their exchange control rules when taking out an international mortgage and can charge exorbitant rates.

The best suggestion for foreign nationals is to find an international mortgage brokerage or international relocation specialist who will be able to offer great mortgages at special low rates, and who has experience dealing with overseas investors. These professionals frequently provide international currency exchange services and allow foreigners to easily invest in property or pay any overseas accounts. For overseas real estate investors who will be engaging in various sales and purchases of real estate over the years, as well as paying for services, invoices, and other accounts related to their properties, an international mortgage and currency exchange broker is definitely the way to go.

Foreign Payment

A foreign investor is required to pay three different taxes on their property, as follows:

THE TITLE WAVE OF REAL ESTATE

- Capital Gains Tax: Capital Gains Tax is charged at 15 percent to a private investor, although a corporation is looking at around 35 percent. This tax is charged on the gain of the sale of the asset. In other words, the difference between the selling price and the actual value of the property. Because the gains and other corresponding taxes aren't known at the time of closing, the 10 percent withholding rule was introduced, although this 10 percent amount often exceeds the actual capital gains tax.
- Income Tax: Income tax for a foreign investor is also between 15 and 35 percent on individuals and corporations, the process being the same as it is in the US. If the property is individually owned, the taxes are much lower, but with LLCs and land trusts, privacy is favored above tax implications. LLCs, however, do enjoy similarly low income taxes, as this type of company is treated as though it doesn't exist in terms of US taxes.
- Gift or Estate Tax: The gift tax applies when a foreigner purchases a property as a gift for another person. This tax can be as much as 45 percent, and the same tax may also be required upon the death of the owner as an estate tax. Some countries have an estate tax treaty with the US, so you will have to find out which clients are exempt from paying these taxes. To get the best of both worlds, foreign investors can establish an LLC or Florida land trust, which could negate the estate taxation.
- Branch Tax (for Foreign Corporations only): For corporations purchasing real estate, there is another tax that many are unaware of called the branch tax. Any additional income received from the purchase of property in the US by a foreign corporation might also be subject to 30 percent branch tax over and above the income and capital gains taxes.

Foreign investors are often faced with confusing rules and regulations when investing in US property. Real estate laws can differ significantly from their home country, making the process complicated and puzzling. The best course of action for a foreign seller or investor to avoid this confusion and ensure their closing process goes smoothly is to work with a US real estate professional or team of professionals when buying or selling property in the US.

The Title Agency and a Foreign Investor

A real estate closing in the US can involve many players. Besides the buyer and seller, there may be realtors working with both sides. Each side might also have a lawyer representing their interests and reviewing contracts. In most cases, there is also a mortgage lender involved, and a title insurance agency to pull it all together.

At Independence Title, we've closed on hundreds of foreign investor transactions, and we speak from experience. Working with a reputable and experienced title insurance agency means that a foreign investor can be assured that the closing process will go smoothly, and all legal obligations will be met. The title agency serves as an impartial player in the closing, collecting documents, researching the property title, and oftentimes holding funds as an escrow agent. It's the job of the title agency to make sure that the closing happens without favoring either the buyer or seller. This is even more important when the buyer is a foreign national, and therefore absent during much of the process.

The title agency often fulfills the role of communicator between all parties, which can be a very valuable service for a foreign investor. The title agent will be able to walk investors through US-specific terminology, rules, and regulations, and answer any questions that come up.

With the right guidance, a foreign investor or seller can understand US real estate terminology and rules, and can experience a smooth closing.

Chapter 16

The Florida Land Trust and Limited Liability Companies (LLCs)

Both local and foreign real estate buyers should be aware of real estate rules and regulations in their target area, so that they can take advantage of them. In Florida, this includes the Florida land trust, which can play an important role in any real estate transaction.

What is a Florida Land Trust?

In Florida, land trusts can be set up by any individual, group of individuals, limited partnership, general partnership, limited liability company (LLC), or a trust service provider. The Florida land trust can be established for a number of reasons, most commonly to secure and protect the asset, as well as to ensure the privacy of the buyers.

To set up a Florida land trust, you start by completing various forms that name your trustee. The company setting up the trust usually provides these forms. In naming the grantor, you can either use your name as the owner or put it under the title company or trust service provider's name. The service provider will be named as trustee of the land trust, and many experts recommend using a company in a different state to further enhance the privacy factor. The trustee has all the fiduciary responsibilities of the trust, and answers to the beneficiaries of the trust, who retain all the ownership rights.

According to Uniform Trust Code (UTC) requirements, the same person cannot be named as the sole trustee and the sole beneficiary of the trust, as the same person cannot hold all equitable titles and all legal titles at the same time. This merger of property interests would make the trust non-existent under the "merger doctrine."

Although considered to be an affordable option, there are still various costs involved. These are in the form of a setup fee, which can range anywhere from $250 to $500, attorney fees for the administration of the trust, including the submission of tax forms and bills (in the case of an irrevocable land trust), as well as yearly fees averaging $300 for maintaining the trust.

How Does the Title Insurance Affect a Land Trust?

Insuring property in a land trust requires the services of an experienced insurance agency or company. **You need to make sure that trustees of your revocable trust are covered under any title insurance policy you bought when you bought real estate.**

Any changes to the beneficiaries or ownership details must be communicated with the insurance company, so that any loss or claim can be processed easily. Title insurance is specifically aimed at Florida land trusts, and offers business premises liability in a separate policy. Ordinary homeowner insurance will not offer adequate protection for land trust-owned property, and must be dealt with separately.

Benefits of Setting up a Florida Land Trust or LLC

Privacy

As we've already established, the main benefit for groups of real estate investors is privacy. Their names are not listed on any public records, as the trustee will be a third party company or bank. The owners will be listed as the beneficiaries of this trust, therefore remaining completely isolated from the real estate. This means that they own a beneficial interest in the trust, this interest being personal property, not real property. Their personal information will be completely confidential, but as far as asset protection from creditors goes, additional protective measures should be implemented, as creditors can still seize beneficial interest. This will be discussed further in the next point.

Privacy becomes increasingly sought after for groups that own a fair amount of real estate in the same area, due to strict code enforcement. Trusts effectively eliminate the possibility for city code enforcement to find the owners, and send them to court for various, often minor, code violations.

Protection from Judgments or Liens

This form of asset protection is not concrete using a Florida land trust alone. Judgments and liens can be held against the beneficial interest, but for the most part, by placing real estate into a land trust, the property can be protected somewhat from personal judgments. This is due to the fact that the owners are not named on the title to the property; therefore, no one knows that they own any property. To offer further protection the beneficiaries can create an LLC to act as the main beneficiary for the trust.

Protection from Title Claims

Similarly, placing property in a land trust will protect the beneficiaries from any title claims that might be field if there is a problem with the title. This usually occurs when a lien is filed against the owner without their knowledge, and if this happens, the owner can be held liable, even if they have title insurance. Land trusts prevent this from happening.

Avoiding Litigation

Suing someone with lots of property, or even just one property, is easy, because attorneys will always look for cases where people have assets (money) involved, making them easy to win. By appearing to be "broke", it is possible to avoid lawsuits and discourage lawyers from taking the case.

Protection from Homeowner's Association (HOA) Claims and Special Levies

Owning a property in a complex means that there are often HOA claims due to maintenance, upgrades, and other unscheduled fees. If the title is held in the owner's name, they are then liable to pay these fees personally. Placing the real estate in a Land Trust means that only this trust or the LLC created (therefore the property itself) is the only recourse for the HOA debts.

Making Non-Assignable Contracts Assignable

The beneficial interest in a trust or LLC is assignable, meaning that the beneficiaries can be changed easily, without changing the title of the property. This is extremely helpful for real estate investors who wholesale real estate and want to purchase bank owned properties. The non-assignable clause is a big stumbling block for investors because it means that the person placing the offer must be the person who closes the sale, with no transfers allowed. A land trust allows flexibility when wholesaling real estate, as the transfer is merely that of the beneficiary, without the property needing to be closed and then resold.

Making Loans Assumable

A non-assumable loan, as far as property is concerned, is when the mortgage of the real estate is due in full upon the sale of the property. This falls under the "Due on Sale" clause of the contract. If, however, the property is held in a Florida land trust or LLC, this clause can be made null and void, as the property is essentially not being sold. The beneficiaries are merely changing. Other benefits include:

112

- The price of the property is not listed in public records.
- You can avoid lengthy and costly probate, as ownership can be easily transferred to spouse, children or other successors.
- The taxes on the property are lower if the price is private.
- Management of the rental property is easier when there is a trustee.
- The negotiation of a sale or purchase is easier with a trust.

How Many Land Trusts Should Be Used

It's possible for many properties to be placed in the same trust, and for investment purposes where the group of benefactors is common to each property, using the same land trust can eliminate a lot of hassle. It will also be cheaper to add properties to the same land trust instead of creating a new one for every new property that the group wants to purchase.

The only instance where a new land trust should be set up is when there are different beneficiaries for each property, or if you wanted to transfer the beneficial interest in one property to another. If two properties were held in the same trust, the beneficial interest could not be transferred from one to the other; so, if this is the aim of your investment, you should use two different trusts. Establishing separate land trusts is not difficult, and although is a bit more costly, it's worth the effort for these purposes.

An important factor to consider when setting up a land trust for real estate investment purposes is that separation of the assets could be an advantage. Let's say a group of buyers invest in six different properties, which are rented out for vacation purposes and long-term rentals. Five of the properties are rented out within a month of being advertised, but one property struggles to secure tenancy. While the first 5 properties are generating income, the final property is standing empty, with mortgage repayments and other bills accumulating. What could happen over a longer period of time, if that final property fails to get a tenant, is that the overdue payments can be accrued from the income of the other properties in the trust.

This option might be suitable in certain instances so that the income can be shared and used across all the properties, but if things ever got to the point where the lien was called in, or a claim was laid against one of the properties, all the other properties would be considered assets of the trust, and could therefore be seized by any creditor. To prevent this from happening, separating assets is the answer. One of the more affordable and effective ways of doing this is to split up the properties into different trusts by categorizing them.

So, in the case above, the vacation properties that earn seasonal income could be held under one land trust, with the long-term rental properties in a different one. Properties that are considered more "problematic" than others should also be separated into a trust of their own to isolate them completely from the others.

Choosing whether or not to combine properties into one Florida land trust can really only be decided by looking at the purpose of your investment, and assessing your real estate portfolio. There are pros and cons to each method.

Using a Third Party Managing Agent to Rent the Property in Trust

Now that the property is in a land trust and all the documents are in order, the next step is to get income from the property. Renting out the real estate is done in the same way as if the property was owned by an individual. The name of the land trust is used on the lease agreement as Lessor, with all income generated being paid into the trust's account.

It's up to the beneficiaries to find a rental agency and instruct the trustee to appoint them as the managing agents for the property. For privacy purposes and to ensure confidentiality, any legal agreements between the agency and the trust will be signed and handled by the trustee. The beneficiaries never have to be involved in the property or be in contact personally with the managing agents.

One of the beneficiaries could step in as the managing agent and oversee the running and maintenance of the property, and if privacy is not an issue then this is acceptable. Setting up a managing agent is more secure, however, and allows for better control, especially when several beneficiaries are involved. The management of the property is easier with a reputable managing agent who can handle complaints, draw up legitimate rental agreements, deal with an HOA and attend meetings if applicable, and perform reference checks on potential tenants.

Managing agents will also be involved in the general upkeep of the property, as advised by the trustee (on behalf of the beneficiaries). Agencies have databases of trusted contractors to perform repairs and maintenance, and they'll contact these companies, process quotes and invoices for payment, and oversee the work done on the property, so that the beneficiaries don't have to be involved.

Selling Property in a Land Trust and Termination of the Trust

One of the objectives of setting up a land trust is to secure ownership when a group of investors want to purchase the same property, thereby becoming co-beneficiaries. In order to sell the property, sub-divide it, or partition off a portion, all the beneficiaries must be in agreement. No partition actions are allowed on properties held in Trust, because the beneficiaries technically don't own the real estate. They own a beneficial interest in the real estate, and if they really wanted out, they would have to sell their beneficial interest to a new party. If this action isn't restricted in the agreement between beneficiaries, they can do this without the consent of the other beneficiaries. In the case of a conflict arising amongst the beneficiaries, it's recommended that joint or co-beneficiary agreements be avoided.

The sole purpose of creating a land trust for real estate investment is to purchase property to resell for a profit, or to sell to a

Florida land trusts can be established for a number of reasons, most commonly to secure and protect the asset.

third party client. The sale of the property is always the ultimate goal. With a Florida land trust in place, the property will easily avoid the double closure involved in purchasing property to transfer to a third party. Instead of needing to foreclose first, incur all the closing costs, and undergo lengthy transfer procedures, you can simply transfer the beneficial interest to the third party, who will then take ownership of the trust, and close the deal. This allows real estate investors to retain 100 percent of their profits. The sale of beneficial interest also has no bearing or impact on lending criteria, and does not violate any form of bank approval.

Foreclosures are also simpler with properties in a land trust. In this case, the trustee foreclosure services like the posting notice of trustee sale, public auctioning, and the trustee deed issuance are taken care of without the beneficiaries being named personally, letting you keep a good name and clean personal credit history.

The typical sale of real estate within a trust all comes down to transferring the beneficial interest. If the new beneficiaries don't want to keep the property in the trust, they can either terminate the trust agreement or wait until the term has ended (if the trust is irrevocable). Generally, Florida land trusts are fully revocable, meaning that termination can take place at any time.

In the instance of an irrevocable land trust, the UTC, states in Section 412(a) that the trust can be terminated when it: "expires pursuant to its terms, no purpose of the trust remains to be achieved, or the purposes of the trust have become unlawful, contrary to public policy, or impossible to achieve." The code does also permit other forms of termination or modification to the trust, which are settled in court, namely when all the parties (i.e., the grantor and all beneficiaries) give their consent.

In the case of an uneconomical trust where the total value is less than $50,000, and outweighs the costs of administration, the trustee may choose to terminate the Trust with notice being given to the beneficiaries. Courts may also consider these grounds for termination, but might appoint a different trustee to manage the trust. If the trust is terminated, the trustee is required to distribute the funds outright and proportionally to the value of the interest of each beneficiary "in a manner consistent with the purposes of the trust." (UTC, Section 414)

By selling property using a land trust, you avoid the hefty transfer taxes that are charged when properties change ownership. Once transfer taxes are implied, this could also result in the actual property taxes being increased as they are scrutinized more closely.

Limited Liability Company (LLC)

Another way to protect and invest in property effectively, without being named on any title deed, is to form an LLC, or limited liability company. This LLC will basically perform in the same way that the land trust does. It's a larger entity containing numerous members, with the name of the LLC being used on the title deed. This protects each member's personal assets and finances from any lawsuits, claims, or liens that might occur, especially if the property is going to be rented out. It must be noted however, that as of April 2010, single-member LLCs are no longer protected by Florida legislature. A creditor can still foreclose on an individual's interest in a single-member LLC.

Rented properties are troubled with potential financial risks, including slip and fall claims, fire-related claims, environmental contamination claims, and various personal injury claims. Instead of these claims resting on the members to personally settle, the income generated by the property in the LLC is used to settle any liens. With a property in an LLC, it still affords some level of privacy, although it's easier for lawyers and private investigators to look up the LLC and find the managing director, managing agent, and other members.

Using an LLC for additional privacy is normally done in conjunction with a land trust, as discussed above, where the LLC's sole purpose is to act as the main beneficiary of a Florida land trust, making it harder for creditors to track down the owners of the trust and thereby protecting the beneficial interest of the trust.

The creation of LLCs allows real estate investors with multiple properties to separate the problematic assets from the premium ones, therefore protecting each asset from the other. It also offers some level of flexibility when it comes to the distribution of profit among the members.

As far as tax is concerned, the LLC is classified as a "pass-through" company, which means that the income it generates is sent through to its owners and then claimed on their personal tax returns. This means that the LLC is only subject to capital gains tax on each member's ownership shares, and not on corporate gains tax as well.

An LLC may be complicated to set up, and costly, and it's easily dissolved if a member dies or wants to leave, but there are certainly great advantages to using it for real estate investing, specifically for asset protection. An LLC will remain one entity, and be held completely separate from your personal finances. Therefore, a creditor laying a claim against the LLC cannot touch your personal finances and assets, even though you own some shares in that LLC. The only assets that can be touched are those of the actual property held in the LLC and the income gained from it, i.e., through rental.

If you're looking at existing LLCs that want to invest in real estate, it's highly recommended that any property be placed in an LLC separate to the main business, so that any liens or claims that might occur from the property, such as a lawsuit from an injured tenant, cannot be used to force a member to sell his/her ownership rights in the business.

Although creating an LLC is a great form of asset protection, it does come with its drawbacks, such as maintenance. The first thing that needs to be done once an LLC has been formed is to ensure that all the forms and documents are professionally drafted, completed, and recorded correctly. This includes the operating agreement, ownership interest documents, and other records. Then, as an LLC is a business entity, annual meetings must be held, and detailed minutes taken.

Why is all this necessary? Well, if there's ever a problem with the LLC, and it's being sued for damages by a tenant, and then the owner of the LLC will need to give a deposition under oath. If there are any problems with the paperwork, it could result in the plaintiff's attorneys being able to "pierce the corporate veil," meaning that they'll be allowed to ignore the liability protection and go after the owner's personal assets. They will no longer distinguish the LLC and owner's personal assets as two separate entities, but see them as "one and the same."

How Does Title Insurance Play a Role?

Coverage for trustees under the title insurance policy depends on when you purchased your real property and the type of title insurance issued for the purchase. For example, starting in 1998, an American Land Title Association homeowner's policy included language that provided for specific coverage of the successor trustee. However, just because you purchased real property after 1998 doesn't guarantee that your title insurance company used a policy that covers the trustees of a revocable living trust, so you need to check this.

In some states, when you purchase a property, you obtain a title insurance policy that covers you for any loss or damage you may sustain in case the property is claimed by someone else, and turns out to not be yours. Among other title issues, the title insurance policy will give you some assurance that you own the property free and clear of other people's claims and rights. When you sell the property, that title insurance does not transfer to your buyer. Given your scenario, your transfer from your name to an LLC may be considered a sale, and the LLC would therefore not be protected under your title insurance policy.

Chapter 17

Rehabbing Residential Real Estate and Remodeling Costs

Rehabbing is one of the areas of real estate investing that makes people very nervous. Where do you start? How do you go about it to ensure a profitable outcome? What costs and time is involved? A fair amount of research is required before you start on your rehabbing venture to find out if this is the way you want to go. If done correctly however, rehabbing residential real estate to flip it can a highly lucrative business to get into, not to mention the sense of achievement that it gives.

The primary goal of rehabbing property is to successfully sell or flip the remodeled home to turn a profit. The majority of homes that are rehab home are those repossessed by the banks. Bank repos, although cheap, are delicate purchases, because there are usually plenty of problems that you are likely to encounter.

Firstly, a bank repo is usually in poor condition as the previous owner would not have maintained or fixed anything on the house due to their financial predicament. Secondly, many owners are bitter and upset about the repossession, which leads them to damage the property. Although you can find gems in amongst the flurry of bank repo homes, careful inspection needs to be done before you make an offer, so that an accurate assessment of the damage can be established.

Many investors have been hard hit due to buying a cheap home only to be inundated with huge repair and renovation costs that they did not plan for. For investors, the key is to purchase a home that is cheap, but that also requires minimal renovation work, or at best, some minor repairs and maintenance.

In the end it all comes down to the costs of the repairs and what repairs are needed, as well as the purchase price of the house and what it can be resold for after the repairs are complete, also known as the after repair value (ARV). The following points should all be considered before you decide to go ahead with rehabbing properties.

Know Repair Estimates Before Making an Offer – Hiring an Inspector

Understanding all the costs involved in the repairs to the house before making an offer is very important. Hiring a professional real estate inspection agency to assess the property should be number one on your "to do" list. The inspection will be thorough and cover all the structural damages as well as cosmetic damages to the home so that you can draw up an accurate budget of the repair costs and decide whether or not the property is worth purchasing.

Once you have received an accurate breakdown of the repairs, you need to deduct this from the ARV, before making an offer to the bank or seller. To work out the ARV, you would need to look at the market value of similar properties in the same area that are in good condition.

Once an inspector has revealed all the damages and possible repairs that need to be made, for example, a termite infestation that needs to be sorted out, or a roof that is badly damaged and on the brink of caving in, you will need to get a contractor out to give you a quote for the repairs. It is preferable to get at least 2 quotes for the repairs, and once you have these; you can determine the overall repair costs.

122

Now that you have the ARV and the total cost of repairs, you will need to deduct the repairs from the ARV to get your base price and then multiply the result by about 65% which is the maximum percentage. If you can lower this, it will be to your advantage as an investor, affording you a better profit in the end.

Estimating the repair costs is not an exact science and even with numerous quotes from contractors, there are still unexpected problems that might be encountered or additional repairs that were not seen upon the initial inspection of the property. It is something that comes with time and experience.

As you approach rehabbing, a minor solution is to add on an additional 10% or 20% to each repair estimate you receive, in order to cover any small, additional expenses that might pop up. Building costs are usually estimated to be 20% more than the actual cost anyway, and any good contractor will set aside an additional amount for overruns.

Knowing the estimated costs also comes down to what materials will be the most beneficial in the resale of the home. Should you replace the damaged kitchen counter top with granite or laminate? What is the difference in the price and how much will it affect the ARV? What will difference be in the cost of repairing a dividing wall, or ripping it out altogether? These aspects all need to be considered and calculated before making an offer on the property.

Best Return on Investment Items and What Will Make the House Sell Faster

Flipping homes generates a good income for real estate investors, but how can you capitalize on this? Well, one way is to ensure that you choose to repair items and renovate areas of the home that will offer the best return. Certain items will make the house sell faster and help to increase the sale price. While it is tempting to do quick fixes and get a home ready as fast as possible, in the long run, it is better to correctly assess the repairs according to what give you the best return on your investment.

Various factors are involved in the return on investment including:

- Time of Year
- Market Temperature
- Location of Home
- Competing Inventory

It is important to stay ahead of the trends and by looking at the basic guidelines that apply to the majority of homes; you can gauge the costs and returns. A good idea is to read the Cost vs. Value Report published by the National Association of Realtors each year in Remodeling Magazine. This features the costs of various home projects and the returns covering 4 regions, and lists the national average.

According to Home Gain's property experts the average return on investment is as follows:

Clean and De-clutter – 973%

This is an important aspect to selling any home. It must be clean and neat with minimal clutter. When renovating, make sure that everything is clean and wiped down before showing prospective buyers and also make sure that all building materials, broken items, and anything else lying around has been cleared away completely.

Lighten and Brighten – 865%

It has been proven that people prefer to buy homes that are light and airy. Ensure that the paint you choose is light in color, that any windows and skylights are clear and free from blockages, use light drapes and keep them open, replace any damaged or broken light bulbs and fix any electrical components that are defective.

Yard/Garden – 426%

This is the first impression that people have of the home, so the yard and garden must be as neat and tidy as the home itself. Planting some brightly colored flowers will really improve the appearance of the yard, as will trim back shrubs and trees. Cut the grass, weed everything, and make it as neat and tidy as possible.

Plumbing and Electrical – 260%

This is important for the electrical and plumbing inspections so ensure that you include repairing plumbing and electrical faults in your estimates. Look for large trees outside with roots growing under the house, as this cause a major plumbing headache later down the line. Also check under bathroom basins and kitchen sinks for uneven wet spots and shower stalls for any signs of leakage. As far as electrical conditions go, the fuse box and breakers should be checked for damage and the age of the electrical wiring and when it was last replaced should be determined. Checking the air conditioning unit is also recommended.

Staging the Home – 251%

After the renovation, staging the home is a well-known aspect of attracting buyers. People like to see what the rooms look like with furniture in it and prefer to get a feel for what each room is used for. You don't have to spend a lot of money on this, and it is perhaps worthwhile to invest in some basic staging furniture, which you will use in every home you flip. Remember that less is more, so choose some basic items like a couch, bed, table and dresser just to make the home look lived in, but not overcrowd it. It is a good idea to get some advice from a professional staging company or interior decorator to achieve the best look.

Kitchen and Bathroom – 168%

Kitchens are often expensive to renovate, due to the costly appliances. If you can avoid replacing these then do so. Instead take care of the cabinetry and counters in kitchens. These need to be updated and modernized, and will have a huge impact on buyers. According to Remodeling Magazine, however, the high-end kitchen renovations do not return as well as the mid or minor remodels, so just creating a neat, modern, blank canvas that people can personalize and customize themselves is the key.

Cabinets can be repainted or resurfaced if the actual cabinets are still in good condition, and countertops do not need to be granite, but a laminate that looks like granite is cheaper and has the same effect. It is worthwhile getting new faucets and making sure there is a sparkling, non-leaky sink. This is the main concern that buyers have about kitchens.

Bathrooms also recoup more than 100% as per the national average, so new flooring, light fixtures, and modern plumbing pays off.

Paint Interior – 148%

Buyers spend a lot of time looking at ceilings. Usually they are looking for signs of leaking, but the last thing you want is for them to be staring at a stained ceiling, or one with cracks. There are some easy repairs for cracks including using fiberglass tape, joint compound and sand. A fresh coat of paint does wonders.

As far as wallpaper is concerned, it is best to get rid of it. Not all buyers like wallpaper, and even those that don't mind it, will probably hate the existing pattern because it is a personal choice. In addition to this, buyers always wonder what is lurking behind the wallpaper, how many layers there are on top of each other, and how easy it will be to remove, so rather do this before putting the house on the market. Likewise, Wall paneling is out dated so paint over this, or remove it.

Flooring and Carpeting – 101%

Hardwood is popular, but expensive, so don't install it, but expose and polish up any that has been hidden away under carpeting for years. Otherwise, carpeting still remains the most popular type of flooring, especially in bedrooms, but choose a light tan color with short pile. Tiled floors are also popular, but avoid tiling out the entire home; instead, just repair or replace a few tiles. When choosing flooring, also take into account the area and how hot or cold it gets, as well as practicality of the location. For example, a home situated right on the beachfront, where lots of sand will inevitably be walked inside, will benefit from an easy-to-clean tiled floor as opposed to carpeting.

Paint Exterior – 76%

Painting the exterior gives the home a new look, and other aspects will all go a long way to selling the home. You should patch cement cracks in sidewalks, plant flowers, resurface asphalt driveways, caulk windows and doors, fix or paint fences, and replace doorknobs and locks. Also take care of the roof. This is a major expense, but people will shy away from buying a home where the roof needs fixing.

One of the newest trends that many homeowners are considering when they make their property purchases are the energy efficiency of the home and how "green" it is. It is worthwhile to incorporate energy saving systems into the home if you are busy repairing that area anyway, and by being able to accurately predict the energy costs for the home, buyers show more of an interest.

Things to Avoid Repairing

Real estate investing is a tough business with very important decisions that will need to be made in terms of the repairs made to the home to rehab it. Although, there is the option of repairing everything in the house, this can be too costly and will not allow you to make much of a profit. There are certain items that you can avoid repairing that will not have a huge impact on the sale of the property or the sale price, but that will save you a lot of time and money.

One of the major things to avoid is structural repair. If you inspect a home only to find that there are problems with the foundation or any other part of the main structure, you should give it a miss. Walls and structural beams as well as roof repairs are expensive and may not be worth repairing. You must

Understanding all the costs involved in the repairs to the house before making an offer is very important.

look at the ARV of the property to determine if you can afford to make these repairs.

The next thing to avoid is going over-the-top with repairs. You should look at the surrounding areas and the neighborhood that the property is located in and repair the home to fit in with the rest of the properties. Do not spend thousands on fitting fancy fixtures and expensive marble entrance halls, when the property is located in a lower income bracket.

One point to note is that if the major structural repairs are avoided, everything that is considered a minor or cosmetic repair should be done, expertly. Avoiding the seemingly insignificant repair work will set you back in the long run, so rather spend the money on new light fittings and on hiring a landscaper to beautify the yard, as this will attract buyers despite the major repairs that might be required.

Avoid replacing what you can repair. This is probably the oldest adage in the book, as far as any form of renovation goes. If you have items that are slightly damaged, it is far more cost effective and easier to simply repair them. This can be said of flooring, windowpanes, and even roof tiles. Re-tiling an entire house may not be necessary if there are just a few tiles chipped or cracked. Rather, replace those few, or repair the cracks and save yourself a lot of time and money.

Another thing you should avoid when rehabbing is to refit a kitchen with new appliances. This is not necessary and all that is really required is a modern, comfortable looking kitchen with solid plumbing and lots of storage. Appliances present a huge cost, and many homeowners will prefer to choose their own new appliances anyway. The same goes for bathrooms. It is not necessary to rip out the bath and shower (unless it is in a really bad way and the bath is lime green for instance!), but rather just replace the faucets and fixtures such as the rails and toilet roll holder. Cabinets and other furniture can be repainted at most, otherwise left as is.

Do I Need a Permit for Repairs?

Yes, when you rehab a property, you will need a permit. Although this is mainly for the major structural, roof, electrical and plumbing repairs, any rehabbing repairs should be made with the correct permits in place, otherwise you run the risk of not having the right to sell the property.

According to all government and city building code law documents, "Permits are required for all new construction, additions, alterations, changes in use and occupancy, movement, enlargement, replacement, repair, equipment, location, removal, and demolition of every building or structure or any appurtenances connected to such buildings or structures. Permits are required for the installation of plumbing, heating, ventilation, central air conditioning, refrigeration, electrical, elevators, escalators, lifts, dumbwaiters, and amusement rides, garages, sheds, decks, swimming pools, awnings, canopies, fences, signs, parking lots, site development and temporary uses/special events."

Permits can be obtained from your local government Department of Building and Planning office or code enforcement office and must be acquired prior to commencement of any property repairs or refurbishments.

Another aspect to permits that you should look into before placing an offer on any property is to find out what renovations where done previously without a permit. If there are any repairs or renovations done to the house without a permit by a previous owner, this will then reflect on the title once you apply for a permit, and the notation will indicate that there was work done without a permit.

To avoid this snafu when you are in the middle on your rehab, rather go down to the nearest government office and ask for the records of when the last permit was applied for on that property and take a look at the last set of plans. You can even access many of the records online. This will save you a lot of trouble later on.

To apply for a building permit, you will need to fill out an application form for each permit you require. For example, if you are making repairs and renovating the bathroom or kitchen you would need to apply for a general building permit, a plumbing permit, and an electrical permit.

Each form is about one page in length and will require the homeowner's personal details, as well as the details and business license of the contractor you have working on the property, so have their details handy. You will be required to describe the type of renovation work to be done and indicate the square footage of any additions. You must also include an estimated cost of the work, but do not overestimate, as you will then be required to pay a higher percentage for the permit than is needed. Lastly, you will need to supply contact details for the designer or architect you are using for any major additions to the property.

Once you have sent back the completed and signed forms you will need to pay the application fee, which differs from place to place. It is best to do this with a money order, instead of a check, because a check will take longer to clear and therefore hold up the entire process.

Once your permits are in place you will need to schedule inspection times with your local city building inspector. This might occur before the permits are finalized, during the rehabbing and again after the completion of the property to ensure that all code procedures and repairs where followed according to building code regulations.

Ensuring that the correct permits are in place will limit your liability and reduce lawsuits that might arise from an unhappy buyer. You don't want anyone getting injured in a home that you resold due to faulty wiring or HVAC installations, and with proper documentation in place, it is less likely for a lawyer to make a case against you for any work done on the house that the buyer is unhappy with.

The permits are also linked to the liability insurance that you should take out on every rehabbing job. If a fire were to break out in a home you rehabbed six years from now, or someone was hurt or killed, this insurance will cover you, however the first thing that they will ask to see is your proof of city building permits, so you must be able to produce these, otherwise coverage will be denied.

Getting Banks to Pay for Major Repairs on Bank Owned Properties

It is not common for the banks to pay for any major repairs to a REO (real estate owned) property they are selling. If anything you can use the inspection report you receive to negotiate a lower purchase price, but as far as repairs go, it is highly unlikely that a bank will agree to pay for anything. You should wait however until your offer has been accepted and insist that a clause is placed in the offer that the closing will be dependent on a thorough home inspection. If any major problems are found, you can then use this to renegotiate the price before closing.

When you submit a low offer, even though the bank has listed the property's price as "firm", furnish it with a detailed reason for the reduced offer and include photographs and cost estimates for the repair to support it. Typically, however, banks usually make major repairs to a badly damaged REO, and bring it back up to local building code standard before putting it on the market, so that they don't tarnish their brand and reputation.

Should you Manage Repairs or Hire a General Contractor to Do It?

Many first-time real estate investors want to project manage their own properties and while this has its perks, it can be time consuming and you run the risk of not overseeing the project thoroughly. Hiring a general contractor on the other hand is more expensive, but on the plus side, you have someone with experience running the project, who is also more familiar with building repairs and construction. Let's look at the pros and cons of each option in more detail:

131

Hiring a General Contractor

Pros:

- A general contractor can oversee more than one rehabbing project at a time.
- They have more experience in the construction and property renovation business.
- They can handle more complex repairs and larger rehabs more effectively.
- They know how to hire excellent contractors for the different aspects of the repair work.
- They can handle the workers, manage problems, fire people if necessary and ensure that the work is running according to schedule.
- They have well-established relationships with other contractors and can probably get good deals for you.

Cons:

- It is going to cost more. (You should expect to pay about 20% to 30% extra)
- On the spot decisions might be made that you do not like or that affect your budget negatively.

Managing the Repairs Yourself

Pros:

- You will save money.
- You can oversee the hiring of contractors and ensure that they all have licenses and certifications.
- You can make on the spot decisions regarding problems or repairs that will help your budget.

Cons:

- It is time consuming and almost impossible if you have more than one rehabbing project, and/or a full-time job.
- You cannot watch the contractors and oversee the work at all hours of the day.

- You must be good at managing people, setting goals and expectations, and hold people accountable when necessary.
- You might not have experience in managing rehabbing projects.
- You might not be good at scheduling workers or understand what areas of construction need to be completed before others can begin.
- It will take longer for the repairs to take place if you only schedule work for when you are available.

As you can see it is more beneficial to hire a general contractor, but if you are available and you want to take on the management side of things on a full time basis, there is nothing wrong with it. There are a few things that you need to keep in mind however, and important questions that you must ask when hiring contractors for your rehabbing project. For example:

- Are you insured, licensed, and/or bonded?
- Do you have workers compensation and insurance? (Ask for copies of the licenses and insurance company information, so that you can verify this)
- How long have you been in the industry?
- How many rehabs or similar repairs have you done?
- Have you worked with a real estate investor before and do you understand what flipping a home entails?
- What kind of breakdown do you provide in your bid and will you create a scope of work?
- How are payments broken up? (It is recommended that you pay the smallest amount up front, then a 25 to 30% payment when you reach the half way mark and then the final payment after the completion of the project, but other breakdowns will work including the milestone method mentioned earlier)

- Do you have your own employees or do you sub-contract? (This is very important, because sub-contractors can hold you liable if the contractor you hire does not pay them)
- Can you give me three references with phone numbers (You must call them!)
- What date can you start and when do you expect the work to be done? (Make sure that there is a final completion date set out on the final signed contract, to ensure that your rehab does not drag on too long)

As the manager of your own rehabbing project you should compare estimates and get at least three bids from contractors you are looking to hire. Make sure that each of them gives you a detailed breakdown of the work that needs to be done so that you can see exactly what you will be paying for.

Remember that flipping homes as a real estate investor is all about fast turnovers and quick sales, and if you spend 6 months rehabbing a property you are going to be losing income for 6 months, plus you will incur holding cost expenses. Therefore it is best to decide on the management of the property according to what will get the rehab completed in the fastest time possible.

In the end it all comes down to what kind of rehab is required. For a few minor repairs, the DIY approach is probably better. You can even do some of these repairs yourself or hire a local handyman to do them. For a major home renovation, however, a general contractor is the way to go.

Make Sure Contractors Have Workers Comp and Insurance

Protecting yourself from possible lawsuits as a real estate investor includes making sure that the contractors you hire are properly insured, and that they have workers compensation (known as workers comp). This will ensure that you are not held liable to pay for any hospitalization or rehabilitation that a worker might require if they are accidentally injured on the site.

As far as licensing is concerned, any contractor with a valid general building contractor license can perform most work on a home including roofing, plumbing and electrical work, but specialty licenses are also issued to electricians and plumbers for their specific field of work.

In order to check the validity of a license you must ask for the contractor's license and pocket ID. You can call the relevant Contractor State License Board to check if the license is valid. You must also check that the pocket license ID matches the company or contractor's name (which should be visible on the side of the company vehicle). It is illegal for a contractor to use someone else's license, just as it is illegal to use someone else's driver's license.

Another reason for choosing a licensed contractor is in the event of a dispute. If the work is valued above a certain amount (for example, it is $300 in California) and you have a problem or dispute, you can make a complaint against the contractor to the State Licensing Board, but if this contractor is not licensed that you will not be able to make a case. This is why it is very important to check the licenses of all contractors you hire.

Aside from the correct licenses being in place, you must verify whether or not your contractors carry workers comp. This compensation is a form of general liability insurance and will protect you from lawsuits if any worker was injured on your property. As extra protection, it is also recommended that homeowners take out an extra liability umbrella insurance policy that covers this as well. This cover will protect your assets in the event of a judgment or liability that falls outside of the limitations of your homeowners insurance.

Workers comp requires monthly premiums to be paid by the contractors, and you should check that these are up to date before hiring a contractor. Ask to see their insurance certification or get them to give you the contact details of their insurance carrier so that you can verify the insurance policy for yourself.

Another form of protection you should not neglect to check is the status of the bonds that the contractor holds. The bonds will protect you from substandard work and repairs that do not comply with local building code regulations. Bonds are classified as a Contractor's License Bond, Performance Bond, Payment Bond, or Contract Bond. These bonds guarantee the completion of the work as agreed upon in the contract drawn up between the contractor and yourself.

Rehabbing Residential Real Estate is Rewarding

Once you have thoroughly assessed all the contractors who you hire to work on your rehab, you can get started on the exciting prospect of remodeling a home for resale. The hard work and effort involved in purchasing a tired, old home, and renovating it to look like new again, is highly rewarding in itself, but when your bank account starts reflecting the profits you make, the success is that much sweeter. Real estate investing in the form of rehabbing properties, is not for the faint of heart, and requires plenty of research, time and energy, but it is a highly lucrative business to get involved in.

Rehabbing residential real estate requires knowledge of the property market and real estate trends, a keen understanding of construction and renovation procedures, budget and cost analysis know-how, and great management skills, as well as an excellent eye for detail. Is this you? Well, armed with the above information, you can now go out and start your rehabbing real estate venture with confidence!

Chapter 18

Investor-Friendly Title Companies

Let's review again the role of a title company and why you need it in the first place. A title company is there to facilitate and coordinate the interests of all parties involved in a real estate transaction, also maintaining the quality of the titles or deeds. They aim to research the title as far back as possible and establish that the chain-of-title is clean and that the property is marketable. In other words, the title company will find out if there are any liens or defects on the title and work to clear these, including any outstanding property taxes, HOA levies, or water services, false affidavits, undisclosed heirs, secret marriages, or invalid divorces. This process of research is called an **abstract of title**.

Once this abstract of title is complete, the title company must then prepare either a title opinion letter or a commitment of title insurance, and send this to both the lender and the prospective buyer. These documents will list the problematic items that need to be corrected in order for the good title to be issued. The title company will work with the list to correct each item and complete all the documents. Once good title is given, the parties can go about exchanging documents and closing the deal with the issuing of the HUD 1 statement. This statement includes all the paperwork for conveying the title, securing the lender, and dealing with other issues such as current leases and rights-of-way, as well as detailing all of the incurred costs.

Over and above the title management duties, title companies are also responsible for drawing up the title insurance policies for the property, which can be either owner or investor title insurance policies or lender title insurance policies. The title insurance companies work closely with real estate agents and help to close sales, giving both parties peace of mind that their important and expensive investment will be insured and protected against any possible claims or lawsuits that may arise. The homeowner or investor title insurance is a once-off payment and lasts for as long as you own the property. There are also no renewal premiums.

How does this apply to using an investor-friendly title company? Well, by making sure that the title company is investor friendly, you can be sure that your title insurance is valid when you make simultaneous or double closings. Many title companies don't offer their services for these kinds of closings, associated with the use of a Florida land trust, and they might tell you that this is not possible or even that it is illegal.

To find investor-friendly title companies, you would need to network with other real estate investors and find out whom they use. The main real estate investor organizations in Florida where you can attend meetings and discover who the big players are, including BREIA (Broward Real Estate Investors Association, NFREIA (Northern Florida Real Estate Investors Association), FINA (Florida Investors Association), BRIC (Boca Real Estate Investment Club) and Distressed REIA (Distressed Real Estate Investors Association).

While many title companies shy away from land trust owned properties and real estate investors, those that are creative and think outside the box will be able to provide ideal, completely legitimate solutions for double and simultaneous closings. This includes directing you how to establish a Florida land trust, so that you also have complete security and anonymity as a property investor. Independence Title is a company that does provide these services in the State of Florida. They offer investor-friendly settlement services.

Wholesaling properties without using an investor-friendly title company will be like banging your head against a brick wall.

A title company is there to facilitate and coordinate the interests of all parties involved in a real estate transaction.

This is because many title companies have no idea about how to work around the assignment limitations on contracts and don't understand how to use Florida land trusts and LLC's to close deals simultaneously. It's not worth trying to explain it to them, so the best thing to do before you find an end buyer or even begin to make an offer on any property, is to first secure a reputable title company that specializes in double closings, simultaneous closings, and that is willing and able to work on deals for real estate investors.

It is very important to ensure that all the title documents are valid, and that they have been legally recorded and safely filed. This eliminates any fraudulent activities that might occur, and prevents problems later on down the line when the property is sold or placed into another Trust, or used for any other purpose.

A company that deals with real estate investors, like Independence Title, always uses Florida land trusts to close deals, as they've discovered that it's the most effective and efficient way to handle investor closings. They specialize in offering real estate professionals the ultimate solution to becoming referral magnets, and give investors the tools and support to thrive in the property market, where many others are struggling.

Chapter 19

Closing Short Sales and Foreclosures

Real estate investments come in various forms, and one of the most profitable forms is that of a short sale or a foreclosure. These two financially beneficial types of property purchases ensure that the buyer is in a good position to resell afterwards, thus making it a top choice for real estate investors. We are going to talk about some of the details in this process but remember when dealing with short sales and foreclosures you must be more careful. There are many issues that can arise when purchasing these types of properties.

Similarities and Differences between Short Sales and Foreclosures

First, let's look at the similarities. Both short sales and foreclosures often sell at a lower than market price. With foreclosures, the property is often damaged and in a poor condition, which makes the price drop. Additionally, the bank is keen to get rid of the property, and will be willing to accept a much lower offer than a traditional seller would accept, usually less than the amount owed on the mortgage. Short sales are also likely to sell for a lower price due to the owners not being able to afford to keep their property any longer. They want the sale to be quick and painless, and are willing to accept lower offers just to secure the sale, which will prevent their property being foreclosed which has negative ramifications for them.

The main difference between a short sale and a foreclosure is that in a short sale the homeowner still owns the property; once the property is foreclosed, it is owned by the bank. In a short sale, the property is also known as a pre-foreclosure. When dealing with this type of sale, however, the buyer is still dealing with the lender or bank during the sale process, as it is the lender who will be taking a loss and not the seller. Basically, in order for a short sale to take place, it must first be approved by the bank or lender, which can sometimes be a time consuming and trying process. Sometimes the bank would prefer to repossess the property anyway, as they might feel they could get more for it as a foreclosure, so there can be various setbacks like this for a real estate investor or buyer.

When looking at the price differences between short sales and foreclosures, it all depends on the bank or lender. Banks only approve the short sale once the seller goes into default; so always make sure that this is the case before you start making offers. Depending on your offer, the bank could counter-offer or reject it outright. They will obviously try to get the best deal possible under the market value, so if they feel that they can get more money for the property by letting it go into foreclosure, they will reject your offer. It is a good idea to find out what similar properties are going for in the same area to ensure that you put in a realistic offer. Another part of this is the negotiation stage, where it is helpful to highlight all the possible costs and expenses that the bank will have to incur if the property should foreclose and making your offer more appealing to them.

Trying to secure a short sale is complicated, and one must avoid using an agent who has no previous experience in short sales. There is the possibility of the short sale taking longer than a foreclosure deal, but this depends on various factors such as when the Notice of Default was filed. After this it can take anywhere from two weeks up to two months for the bank to respond to the Offer Agreement.

The most accurate way of comparing the two, would be to say that buying a short sale is much more unpredictable than buying a foreclosure. There are benefits and disadvantages to this method, but generally the decision to buy a short sale over a foreclosure would simply be that the buyers love the house, or that the price is too good to pass up on.

So, now that you have a good idea as to the similarities and differences between the two options, let's dive into more detail about short sales and what you would need to look for, what the benefits are, and how the process works.

What to Look for when Buying a Short Sale or Foreclosure

There are various factors that one should research and analyze when deciding to buy a short sale or a foreclosure. Factors like the type of property, the size of the property and the land size, the area the property is situated in (the neighborhood), the price, and the resale value all influence the sale. Let's have a look at these items in more detail:

Type of Property

Looking at the type of property is important when choosing a short sale or foreclosure. Is it a house that might require a lot of maintenance and refurbishing to bring it up to standard? Is it an apartment that requires little maintenance, but where association maintenance is payable on a monthly basis? Is it a condo, cottage, log cabin, semi-detached, or double story? All these will play a role in the price and resale value of the property.

For instance, if the property is a single story cottage on a large plot, there is a lot of potential to build on, making it a double story and perhaps extend the house to include more bedrooms, an entertainment area or add on a guesthouse or small cottage. This

143

type of property would offer an excellent resale value and would be highly profitable for any investment buyer.

Size

The size of the property is a factor that should be considered when purchasing a short sale or foreclosure. As the above example indicates, a small sized property offers the buyer a great opportunity to extend the home, with the intention of increasing the value.

The size also plays a role in determining the best price according to the number of bedrooms offered, if there is an entertainment room, and the number of bathrooms. The comfort factor is important to a buyer, not only if they are going to resell the house, but also when it comes to letting the property out to tenants.

Area

Looking at the price of the property is not all a buyer should be concerned with. It is the long-term goal that should be focused on, in other words, the resale value or the rental value. A property in a low-income neighborhood will not secure the same monthly rental as the same size property in a high-income neighborhood. Buyers should investigate the market values pertaining to rentals and resale properties in the area they are looking at before deciding to go ahead with submitting an offer.

Price

The price is the most obvious factor to look at with any short sale or foreclosure. The price must be worth the effort of going through with a short sale, and if there is a chance to purchase a regular property for the same or similar price, then this would obviously be the better option. If you are intent on going for a short sale, then be aware that you might need to raise your offering price. Haggling over prices is what the short sales tend to become, and the seller might push you to increase your price so that the bank or lender approves the short sale. The bank might also counter-offer if

144

they feel they are losing too much money with the property and want to cut their losses.

Property investors can capitalize on this further by doing some investigation into the homeowner's mortgage company and determining how much percentage of loan forgiveness they are willing to accept. If a certain company has a history of agreeing to short sales in which 15 percent of the loan is forgiven, then you could use this to get the homeowner's to push down the price.

With a foreclosure, you are likely to find lower prices than with short sales, but if a slightly higher offer was made than the asking price, the property could be prevented from going to auction. If it goes to auction you have no say as to what the end purchase price will be.

Resale Value

For property investors, the resale value is the most essential aspect of the process. It encompasses all the other points above, so before even making an offer you have researched the size, area, market values, and property type to determine whether you will be able to make a profit from reselling the property.

A complete home inspection is vital for this purpose, as various renovations will push up the investment you make on the property, but also affect the resale value. You should have some ideas in mind after viewing a property about what changes, alterations, renovations or maintenance you would make to the property so that you can research how much these changes will increase the resale value by, also taking into account the area, size, and property type.

Benefits of a Short Sale

There are various benefits to buying a short sale property, just as there are benefits to buying foreclosed ones. You will need to make a list of the pros and cons regarding the property and do a comparative analysis to make the right decision for you based on the specific property you are interested in. Following are just some of the advantages of choosing a short sale.

Condition

With many foreclosures, the owners tend to damage the property intentionally to try and get back at the bank, thus lowering its value, however with a short sale property; the owners still reside in the home and will not be likely to trash it.

Additionally, with a foreclosed home that stands empty, it is more vulnerable to vandalism and prone to squatters, especially in the poorer neighborhoods. Choosing a short sale will relieve you of this problem.

This said it is always advisable to do a CMA (Comparative Market Analysis) to determine the fair market value so that you can make a realistic offer to the bank, which they will be more likely to accept. Once you get to the escrow stage, you should still do a very thorough home inspection to determine any issues or damages to the home. Damages are not necessarily due to intentional damage, but could simply due to neglect because of the financial strains on the current homeowners.

Profitability

Many people benefit from a short sale in terms of the profits.

- The buyer is the first person that comes to mind, as the entire aim of the purchase is to make a profit, either through the resale of the property at a higher price, or through the rental of the property. Aside from this, the future taxation of this type of property could be significantly reduced by the tax assessor, since the buyer purchased the property below the market value. Ultimately the buyer's mortgage payments will be less.

146

- The listing and buying agents all benefit from the short sale, even though it could mean a slightly lower commission. At the end of the day, they still get paid to sell and market the property.
- Another person who profits is the new buyer's lender for the short sale property. The short sale means that a new loan will be generated giving the lender new revenue and this also includes the underwriter and loan processor.
- The appraiser also profits from a short sale, as they are called out by the new lender to perform an appraisal on the property. They can charge anywhere from $250 to $650 for this.
- If a mortgage broker was involved in the buyer's loan, then they receive points on the loan.
- The title company also benefits as they are going to be doing the title search and issuing an owner's and maybe even a lender's title policy to the new buyer.
- In some areas a property must be reassessed upon sale, and in this case a county tax assessor will also profit from the sale as they continue to collect property taxes on a regular basis. This could be at a higher assessment value depending on the resale value. Likewise, a tax consultant and a CPA can also profit from this transaction as there might be tax implications due to the debt forgiveness.
- Along the same lines, the Internal Revenue Service (IRS) can even benefit if a 1099 is issued to the seller making them liable for taxation on the short sale.
- If a third-party escrow service, separate from the title company, is used, they will also profit from the short sale, as they get paid by the lender. Their fee is sometimes split between the lender and the buyer.
- Real estate lawyers should be consulted before any short sale agreement is entered into, which means that they profit from

the short sale too. Specialist short sale lawyers will charge more for their ability to negotiate short sales effectively.

- Finally, insurance companies profit from a short sale for insuring the new buyer and the new home. The individual insurance agent also earns a fee on the homeowner's insurance policy.

Downsides of Short Sales

While short sales are beneficial for many reasons, there are also some disadvantages to short sales, which you should be aware of and also research before making a final decision.

The Length of Time It Takes to Close

Ironically, the name short sale does not necessarily mean that the time it takes to close this type of property transaction will be short and hassle free. It can take an extremely long time to close as the process gets dragged out by the bank.

There is a Qualification Required

Most homeowners who are in financial trouble don't realize that they cannot just start a short sale process as a seller. You have to actually qualify for a short sale. To qualify, a letter of hardship should be presented to the bank, in which there is proof that the homeowner has no equity and that they cannot pay the difference between the existing loan and the current market sale price.

All Lien Holders Have to Agree

Before a short sale process is started a buyer must check to see if there are any additional mortgages on the property. Remember that all parties involved in the property must agree to the short sale going ahead and if there is one lien holder who decides that they are not willing to accept the loss that a short sale could ultimately bring them, they can block the sale. It could happen that the sale price of the home does not cover the second mortgage, which means that that particular lien holder will not get paid. This could leave the buyer in a state of limbo as the wait for an answer, so it is imperative that you check this before making an offer on any short sale.

The banks are notorious for making the short sale process as difficult and tiresome as possible. While sending counter offer after counter offer to try and get the best price they can from you and recoup some of their losses, they could also be continuing to get other offers from interested buyers. While many view this as unethical, it is done, nonetheless. This means that even though a prospective buyer might have spent a few thousand dollars on home inspections, title searches, and appraisals, they could get dropped at the last minute in favor of someone with a better offer. For this reason, when you look at the listing price of a short sale, don't assume that this will be the actual price you pay. The banks could be looking for a lot more. At the same token, you might not get a counter offer from the bank. Instead they will simply reject your offer if it is too low right at the beginning. Sometimes they just won't reply to you.

The Process of a Short Sale

Many people assume that the process of securing a short sale is easy, when in fact it is far from it. Remember that you'll be negotiating and dealing directly with the bank, even though the homeowner technically still owns the property. The bank is the one who will be taking the loss, so it is imperative that you deal with them in a cordial, professional manner and always be prepared. However, the bank will have already done their homework into short selling a property by looking at its PSA (Pooling Servicer Agreement) and determining if it will make more money through a foreclosure or short sale.

Although it's hard, there are ways to get the bank to accept your offer and here are the main pointers to keep in mind:

- First, don't ever argue with the bank – even if they are wrong. It is best to give them exactly what they want to ensure that they will give you what you want – the house you are after!

- Return any and all documents as promptly as possible. Even if you think you have already signed a particular document, read it through thoroughly and sign it again. Usually the banks will send you forms including an arm's length affidavit, the short sale listing addendum or the short sale contract which are often edited and changed by the bank's lawyers as the process unfolds, so be amenable and simply sign and resend the latest version as soon as you receive it. Additionally, if the bank requires anything else from you such as a payroll stub or latest bank statement, send this information through to them immediately or to the agent who is handling the short sale.

- Just like making sure that you send documents through in a timely manner, ensuring that they are complete, is just as important. Similarly, when the banks require documentation from you such as tax returns or bank statements, ensure that you send through the full-length detailed version with your loan number clearly marked on each and every page. Many people make the mistake of assuming that the bank will be ok with the shortened versions of documents, and this results in them requiring clarification and in turn dragging the process out even further. On HUD's, it is important that you include both the buyer's and the seller's names, and sometimes they prefer you to give them the junior lien holder's name too. A good short sale agent will know precisely how to complete the HUD so that the banks are 100% happy.

- When making an offer, do your research thoroughly to ensure that you come in with a reasonable, fair price. Do not lowball and always justify your offer with a CMA (Comparative Market Analysis) of the property, which your agent can perform and send through to the bank. Sometimes the bank will tell you that they want to get a higher price for the property based on the BPO. BPO stands for Broker Price Opinion; this is a controversial process by which a broker will perform an evaluation on the property to present its market value. Some argue that these BPO Agents are too inexperienced to give an accurate valuation and tend to undervalue properties. By offering a CMA, you can get around the banks simply telling you that your offer is too low, if it is, in fact, fair.

- Make sure that you give the bank, your documentation, as a buyer. This will show the bank that you are committed to selling. The buyer's agent should send over an earnest money deposit, as well as a preapproval letter, which should be signed and dated by the buyer's lender within the past thirty days. You should also include your latest bank statements.
- If you want to make certain that your offer will be accepted to begin with, you should find out if the seller is in official default. If they are not even at this stage yet, it can take a long time while the banks negotiate with the seller to even get approved for a short sale. If the bank thinks that it can get more money by foreclosing, then they will reject the short sale and you will have wasted time and money for nothing. Even if you see a short sale advertised by an agent, this does not necessarily mean that the bank or lender has signed off on this.

How Long Can a Short Sale Negotiation Last?
The length of time it takes to close a short sale, depends on a number of factors, including the price, the willingness of the banks or lenders to go ahead with the sale, when the Notice of Default was

filed, the backlog of foreclosure that the bank has, how much documentation the seller has already submitted and if any other documentation, assessments, or research is required.

Banks and lenders can take anywhere from two weeks to several months to even respond to the initial short sale purchase offer. Most experienced short sale agents recommend that you give the lender a deadline, but it is difficult to say if this actually makes a difference at all. Also, if the bank or lender has not yet approved the short sale, it isn't worth making a deadline, because it could take several months for the bank to even come to an agreement with the seller. This means that there isn't even a guarantee that the short sale will go through.

Another item that can significantly lengthen the time it takes a short sale to go through is if there is a second lender with a stake in the property, as their needs will have to be discussed and satisfied before the short sale can be agreed upon.

Taking into account the length of time the banks generally take to look at short sale offers, it is best to keep looking at various other properties and if you happen to find another one that you like which is a fairly good price, and that will be easier to close, you should go that route. Some people prefer to pay a bit more for a property if they can circumvent the endless waiting game that short sales tend to be. With this in mind, ensure that the short sale agent drafts your agreement in such a way that gives you flexibility to pull your offer if you find something else.

One of the recommended ways to speed up the process, however, is to enter the HAFA, which is the Home Affordable Foreclosure Alternatives federal program designed to help the buyer and the seller. One of the features that this program offers is the creation of a timeline to work towards, that holds mortgage lenders accountable. There are cases where short sales have closed in thirty days or less through the HAFA program, but the general consensus is that it takes about fifty-eight days.

Is It Best to Let an Attorney Negotiate a Short Sale?

Although it is not completely necessary to let an attorney negotiate a short sale, it is important to get their advice when it comes to the legal aspects of short sales and to give you more insight into the negotiation process if this is something new to you. To handle the negotiation side of things, you would normally hire an experienced short sale agent, as this is their area of expertise.

A lawyer who is experienced in short sales, can be very useful to have to ensure that everything is handled by the books and is above board from a legal perspective. You could also find that it is not necessary to hire an independent attorney to advise you about your short sale, but many short sale specialists have an in-house lawyer for this specific purpose. This lawyer could be called a professional loss mitigation negotiator and they will work to help you get a short sale approval going through all the correct channels, assisting with documentation and the drafting of letters to the bank.

It is possible in some states, such as Florida, for the lenders to try and recoup some of the money they have lost due to a short sale or a foreclosure and will obtain a deficiency judgment against the seller. If this happens you will definitely require the services of a short sale lawyer or mitigation negotiator, otherwise you could potential face years of trying to pay back your former lender or worse, a third-party debt collection agency that the lenders have hired.

As a buyer, one of the reasons it is best to hire a lawyer, is that the bank you are trying to negotiate the short sale with, has a legal team and the best lawyers on staff. They won't hesitate to find the loopholes and put the squeeze on you if they get the chance to. Laws also change constantly, making it more difficult to negotiate a short sale from a legal standpoint. You should be hesitant to doing the short sale yourself, and even if you have a real estate agent handling things for you, nothing replaces the legal advice you get from a professional short sale lawyer.

To successfully negotiate and close a short sale with the least amount of hassle, it is always advisable to hire a specialist team including a professional short sale agent, lawyer and title company. This team effort is always your best bet.

Using Real Estate Investors or Agents for a Short Sale

Before embarking on a short sale, you should consider using a short sale agent or contacting a real estate investor to handle the legalities and complex property details for you. Experience goes a long way in short sales, especially when dealing with difficult banks and lenders, so make sure that you find an agent with a good reputation for short sales.

You will find that some agents turn down short sales because they have had bad experienced with them previously. Short sales do require more work on the agent's side of things, plus they might not get their usual commission, due to the banks already taking a loss. Some lenders are not willing to pay the 5 or 6% commission. Aside from hiring a skilled agent or real estate investor, you should also find out if the listing agent is experienced with short sales as this can help to expedite the process and result in a much easier transaction.

Dealing with a professional short sale agent can mean all the difference in getting a home in poor condition that took forever to close and where you had to raise your price drastically, to getting an amazing deal on a well maintained home in a good area that closed with very little hassle. It is important to deal with well-educated, reputable agents who have a sound history with short sales and plenty of experience.

When Would You Choose a Foreclosure?

Although short sales might be beneficial for many reasons, buying a foreclosed house could prove to be the better option. It really depends on the buyer and what cash is available to start with. For instance, you would choose the foreclosure option if you had the cash on hand and you were looking for a faster sale.

154

Choosing a foreclosure is risky do to the high possibility for damage and vandalism to the property, but you can find many in fairly good condition that are well below the market price. If your main concern is profitability, then a foreclosure is your best bet, but if you are more interested in stability, a short sale is the way to go, as this offers more information about the property. The best way to profit from a foreclosure is to look for a long-term tenant so that you can earn a good residual income from it. This is mostly necessary during economically unstable times when the property market is volatile.

If you did want to renovate the property in order to resell it, this is possible, but you should not spend too much money on this. Before making an offer, work out what renovations you want to do and what is necessary to bring it up to a great resale value. Make sure that this will cost between 5 and 10 % of the sale price and no more, otherwise the property becomes a liability.

Benefits of Buying a Foreclosure

Even though it gets a bad rap, there are certain benefits to buying a foreclosed home, where a short sale may actually provide more problems.

They Sell at a Much Lower Price
Foreclosed homes provide the perfect opportunity to purchase a home at a very cheap price. They are generally about 30% cheaper than non-distressed houses of the same size and type. You can find foreclosures that are labeled as "move-in ready" which are still sold at a reduced price and very worthwhile.

The Buyer Can Negotiate the Price and Closing Costs
Unlike a short sale, where the bank has the final say regarding the price and where closing costs might be high, a foreclosure is already listed as such, which means that you can

negotiate the price and the closing costs. The bank will want to get rid of this property as soon as they can, and will look at any offer, even before the property goes to auction.

The Process is Faster

The amount of time it takes to close a foreclosure property is much faster than a short sale. This is because less time will be spent negotiating, convincing, and dealing with the banks, there are no approvals to wait for, and everything is set out for a smooth transaction.

Disadvantages of Buying a Foreclosure

Although many people prefer the simpler process of buying a foreclosed property and not having the hassle of negotiating with the homeowners as well as the lenders, there are other disadvantages to it.

Cash Payments

A foreclosed property goes to auction where you will be required to purchase the property outright in cash or at least a large percentage in cash, which can be a problem for some buyers.

Condition

By the time a property gets to the foreclosure stage, it is usually in fairly poor condition, as it has not been looked after for years, and has more than likely been standing empty for a long period of time. There could be rodent and insect infestations, which would cost you a lot of money to fix, and there could be various other damages that you do not see or know about until after you have purchase the property.

Most homeowners are bitter about their home going into foreclosure and before they have to move out, many of them damage the property on purpose to try and get back at the banks. They break fences, smash walls, makes holes in the ceiling, rip up carpets, break tiles, and basically make the house unlivable, so that the buyer has no choice but to completely renovate the house. This is perfect for a handyman type, or if you see the potential to transform the home into something completely different. For example, you might see the potential in a house to make it into a two-storey home, in which case you wouldn't care if the roof was damaged and the ceiling full of holes, because you would tear it down anyway.

Structural Problems

Sometimes foreclosures can be riddled with problems from plumbing issues, to infestations, to cracked walls, and more, and sometimes there are even liens against a property, which most property investors at auction do not bother researching. It is imperative that you find out about the property before the auction so that you know what is wrong with it and if it is worth even buying.

Closing the Sale

At the end of the day, when all is said and done, the closing of any property transaction, whether it is a short sale or a foreclosure is to ensure that both parties are happy. The seller or lender is happy to get rid of the property, which is causing a financial strain, and the seller is happy to get the property at a cheaper price, even if they have to fix it up a bit.

Once all the little items have been ironed out and both parties are happy, the Purchase Agreement is drawn up, the property goes into escrow and the rest of the process is quite simple and straightforward.

As a property investor or buyer looking at a cheap option, both foreclosures and short sales have their pros and cons, and to determine which avenue is for you, you will firstly need to look at what you can offer, how patient you are, how flexible you are, and what your end goal is, whether it is to resell, rent out on a long term basis, or renovate and market it as a vacation rental. In either case, certain processes will need to be followed including getting a reputable lawyer, experienced agent, and excellent title company to ensure that your property transaction goes ahead as easily and smoothly as possible.

Chapter 20

Internal Revenue Service (IRS)

This chapter will dive into all of the tax and IRS jargon you need to know and understand when buying or selling real estate, and title insurance. We will look into how the IRS views this type of investing. (As with each topic in this book we suggest you consult with your accountant, financial advisor or attorney before making any type of investment especially buying and selling real estate.)

The Big Debate about Title Insurance

So long as mortgage interest is deductible, borrower payments for services required by lenders to reduce their risk, including **mortgage insurance** and **title insurance**, should also be deductible. Under IRS rules, however, premiums were not deductible until 2007, when Congress granted the privilege to borrowers with adjusted gross incomes of $100,000 or less. It was later extended through 2011. What will come in the future, in regard to protection and title insurance, remains to be seen.

Title Insurance Should Be Deductible

Title insurance premiums on a policy that protects the lender only should be deductible, but aren't. The same is true of expenses billed to the borrower, which are incurred by a lender in connection with a loan, such as a

Buying and selling real estate in today's market is a smart and profitable investment.

credit check or appraisal. The IRS says that they aren't deductible because the borrower receives a service for them, but this is a fiction. The lender requires these services as a condition for granting the loan, and they provide little or nothing of value to the borrower beyond the loan itself. Furthermore, if the lender elects to cover these expenses in the interest rate or points, they are fully deductible.

What You Can and Cannot Deduct

To deduct expenses of owning a home, you must file Form 1040 and itemize your deductions on Schedule A (Form 1040). If you itemize, you cannot take the standard deduction.
This section explains what expenses you can deduct as a homeowner. It also points out expenses that you cannot deduct. There are four primary discussions: real estate taxes, sales taxes, home mortgage interest, and mortgage insurance premiums. Generally, your real estate taxes, home mortgage interest, and mortgage insurance premiums are included in your house payment.

Your House Payment

If you took out a mortgage (loan) to finance the purchase of your home, you probably have to make monthly house payments. Your house payment may include several costs of owning a home. The only costs you can deduct are real estate taxes actually paid to the taxing authority, interest that qualifies as home mortgage interest, and mortgage insurance premiums.

Some nondeductible expenses that may be included in your house payment include:

- Fire or homeowner's insurance premiums
- The amount applied to reduce the principal of the mortgage

Minister's or Military Housing Allowance

If you're a minister or a member of the uniformed services and receive a housing allowance that is not taxable, you still can deduct your real estate taxes and home mortgage interest. You do not have to reduce your deductions by your nontaxable allowance.

Nondeductible Payments

You cannot deduct any of the following items:

- Insurance (other than mortgage insurance premiums), including fire and comprehensive coverage, and title insurance
- Wages you pay for domestic help
- Depreciation
- The cost of utilities, such as gas, electricity, or water
- Most settlement costs
- Forfeited deposits, down payments, or earnest money

Real Estate Taxes

Most state and local governments charge an annual tax on the value of real property. This is called a real estate tax. You can deduct the tax if it's based on the assessed value of the real property and the taxing authority charges a uniform rate on all property in its jurisdiction. The tax must be for the welfare of the general public, and not be a payment for a special privilege granted or service rendered to you.

Deductible Real Estate Taxes

You can deduct real estate taxes imposed on you. You must have paid them either at settlement, closing or to a taxing authority (either directly or through an escrow account) during the year. If you own a cooperative apartment, see *Special Rules for Cooperatives,* later.

Where to Deduct Real Estate Taxes

Enter the amount of your deductible real estate taxes on Schedule A (Form 1040), line 6.

Real Estate Taxes Paid at Settlement or Closing

Real estate taxes are generally divided so that you and the seller each pay taxes for the part of the property tax year you owned the home. Your share of these taxes is fully deductible if you itemize your deductions.

Division of Real Estate Taxes

For federal income tax purposes, the seller is treated as paying the property taxes up to, but not including, the date of sale. You (the buyer) are treated as paying the taxes beginning with the date of sale. This applies regardless of the lien dates under local law. Generally, this information is included on the settlement statement you get at closing.

You and the seller each are considered to have paid your own share of the taxes, even if one or the other paid the entire amount. You can each deduct your own share, if you itemize deductions, for the year the property is sold.

Example: You bought your home on September 1. The property tax year (the period to which the tax relates) in your area is the calendar year. The tax for the year was $730, and was due and paid by the seller on August 15. You owned your new home during the property tax year for 122 days (September 1 to December 31, including your date of purchase). You figure your deduction for real estate taxes on your home as follows:

- Enter the total real estate taxes for the real property tax year: $730
- Enter the number of days in the tax year that you owned the property: 122

162

- Divide line 2 by 365: .3342
- Multiply line 1 by line 3. This is your deduction. Enter it on Schedule A (Form 1040), line 6: $244

You can deduct therefore $244 on your return for the year if you itemize your deductions. You are considered to have paid this amount, and can deduct it on your return even if, under the contract, you did not have to reimburse the seller.

Delinquent Taxes
Delinquent taxes are unpaid taxes that were imposed on the seller for an earlier tax year. If you agree to pay delinquent taxes when you buy your home, you cannot deduct them. You treat them as part of the cost of your home.

Escrow Accounts
Many monthly house payments include an amount placed in escrow (put in the care of a third party) for real estate taxes. You may not be able to deduct the total you pay into the escrow account. You can deduct only the real estate taxes that the lender actually paid from escrow to the taxing authority. Your real estate tax bill will show this amount.

Refund or Rebate of Real Estate Taxes
If you receive a refund or rebate of real estate taxes this year for amounts you paid during the year, you must reduce your real estate tax deduction by the amount refunded to you. If the refund or rebate was for real estate taxes paid for a prior year, you may have to include some or all of the refund in your income.

Items You Cannot Deduct as Real Estate Taxes
The following items are not deductible as real estate taxes.

Charges for Services

An itemized charge for services to specific property or people is not a tax, even if the charge is paid to the taxing authority. You cannot deduct the charge as a real estate tax if it is:

A unit fee for the delivery of a service (such as a $5 fee charged for every 1,000 gallons of water you use)

A periodic charge for a residential service (such as a $20 per month or $240 annual fee charged for trash collection)

A flat fee charged for a single service provided by your local government (such as a $30 charge for mowing your lawn because it had grown higher than permitted under a local ordinance)

Sales Taxes

Generally, you can elect to deduct state and local general sales taxes instead of state and local income taxes as an itemized deduction on Schedule A (Form 1040). Deductible sales taxes may include sales taxes paid on your home (including mobile and prefabricated), or home building materials if the tax rate was the same as the general sales tax rate.

If you elect to deduct the sales taxes paid on your home, or home building materials, you cannot include them as part of your cost basis in the home.

Home Mortgage Interest

This section gives you basic information about home mortgage interest, including information on interest paid at settlement, points, and Form 1098, Mortgage Interest Statement. Most homebuyers take out a mortgage (loan) to buy their home. They then make monthly payments to either the mortgage holder or someone collecting the payments for the mortgage holder. Usually, you can deduct the entire part of your payment that is for mortgage interest, if you itemize your deductions on Schedule A (Form 1040). However, your deduction may be limited if:

- Your total mortgage balance is more than $1 million ($500,000 if married filing separately)
- You took out a mortgage for reasons other than to buy, build, or improve your home.

If either of these situations applies to you, you will need to get Publication 936. You also may need Publication 936 if you later refinance your mortgage or buy a second home.

Refund of Home Mortgage Interest

If you receive a refund of home mortgage interest that you deducted in an earlier year and that reduced your tax, you generally must include the refund in income in the year you receive it. The amount of the refund will usually be shown on the mortgage interest statement you receive from your mortgage lender.

Deductible Mortgage Interest

To be deductible, the interest you pay must be on a loan secured by your main home or a second home. The loan can be a first or second mortgage, a home improvement loan, or a home equity loan.

Mortgage Insurance Premiums

You may be able to take an itemized deduction on Schedule A (Form 1040), line 13, for premiums you pay or accrued during 2011 for qualified mortgage insurance in connection with home acquisition debt on your qualified home.

Mortgage insurance premiums you paid or accrued on any mortgage insurance contract issued before January 1, 2007, are not deductible as an itemized deduction.

Qualified Mortgage Insurance

Qualified mortgage insurance is mortgage insurance provided by the Veterans Administration, the Federal Housing

Administration, or the Rural Housing Administration, and private mortgage insurance (as defined in section 2 of the Homeowners Protection Act of 1998 as in effect on December 20, 2006).

Prepaid Mortgage Insurance Premiums

If you paid premiums that are allocable to periods after 2011, you must allocate them over the shorter of:

- The stated term of the mortgage, or
- Eighty-four months, beginning with the month the insurance was obtained.

The premiums are treated as paid in the year to which they were allocated. If the mortgage is satisfied before its term, no deduction is allowed for the unamortized balance.

Exception for Certain Mortgage Insurance

The allocation rules, explained above, do not apply to qualified mortgage insurance provided by the Department of Veterans Affairs or Rural Housing Service.

Chapter 21

Transactional Funding

If you've a signed contract and are wholesaling your transaction to an end buyer, and don't have the funds to fund the first transaction, you'll need transactional funding. Transactional funding is perfect for bank-owned properties and short sales that you're selling to an end buyer.

Since banks don't allow assignable contracts, you're going to need to schedule a simultaneous or double closing with your end buyer. Double closings, also known as simultaneous closings, allow you to schedule two back-to-back closings for the same property on the same day. You'll need to have a source of funds to pay for the first transaction. This is where transactional funding (also known as same-day funds) is needed.

If you're a real estate investor and you have a closing that needs transactional funding, then we may be able to find the funding for your transaction. However, **you must use our title company for your closing to be considered for this program, and follow the criteria below.**

How Does Transactional Funding Work?

If you're looking to simultaneously close a bank-owned property, you'll have two contracts and two closings. The first contract is between the bank (seller) and you (buyer). The second contract is between you (seller) and your end buyer (buyer). The end buyer is the person that will ultimately be the long-term owner of the property.

Example of Transactional Funding for a Simultaneous or Double Closing

A – Bank

B – You

C – End Buyer

You have a contract with the bank to purchase a bank-owned property at $40,000 (first contract). This is known as the A-B transaction.

You market this property to your cash buyers and find a buyer at $50,000. You sign a contract with this buyer, you being the seller and them being the buyer (second contract). This is known as the B-C transaction.

The difference between the two contracts (after deducting closing costs) is your profit, which you walk away with at the closing. We recommend that your contract with your end buyer contain a clause stating that the end buyer will pay all closing and acquisition costs. This is important, because you want to ensure that you have a net profit number that won't be substantially reduced by the double closing costs. You should always pass these costs on to the end buyer when wholesaling a property (if you can).

Double Closings

Since there are two contracts, there are two closings. This means that you'll pay double closing costs. There are ways to avoid paying double closing costs, like using an entity such as a land trust or an LLC. There are advantages and disadvantages to using these methods. We advise that you consult with your attorney or CPA for advice on the type of entity and its merits. Also, please note that land trusts that are common in Florida might not be legal or common in other states.

What are the Fees for Transactional Funding?

The transactional funding fees are usually range from $795 to two percent of the funded amount, depending on the investor that is available to fund your deal. There is usually a minimum transactional funding fee of $750, which will be added as a closing cost to your HUD-1 statement.

What if I Find an End Buyer?

You should always take a deposit from your end buyer that is at least twice the amount of your initial deposit, and you should always accept only cleared funds, like a cashier's check or wire transfer directly to the title company or attorney. It's your responsibility to provide both contracts to the title company or attorney, and to clearly label all cashier's checks and wires with the property address. It's also your responsibility to communicate with the title company about the transaction to make sure the closing is handled properly.

Where Do We Provide Transactional Funding?

Our investors will provide transactional funding for properties that are located in South Florida. Our investors transactional fund on wholesale properties in Miami-Dade County, Broward County, Palm Beach County, and St Lucie County. Since we are based in Fort Lauderdale, we prefer properties that are within a ninety-minute driving distance. Each transaction needs to be analyzed by us before our investor will provide transactional funding.

Chapter 22

The Title Wave of Fraud

Now that you've learned the foundations of what it means to talk titles and title insurance, it's time to talk about another important topic in title insurance – **fraud**. Let's start with something I've been saying throughout the book – it's very important to know your title company and have a good working relationship with them. It's also a good idea to know who the principals of the company are, since you're depositing your escrow funds with this company. Doing so will minimize the risk of title insurance fraud. Fraud has become a major problem in the industry, and will certainly derail your closing process. It may also cost you a lot of time and money, so it's a good idea to be on top of any fraudulent activity, and stop the problem before it starts.

The most common type of fraud is where the title company or attorney "dips" into the escrow account in order to cover short falls. Any principal of an escrow account can withdraw funds from that account, so it can be very tempting for someone with a criminal mind. Even legitimate individuals with no criminal intent can get in over their head by borrowing from their escrow account to make payroll or pay rent. If they're a little short for the month, it can be tempting to dip into the escrow account and then pay it back from future anticipated fees. The problem lies with the fact that once they make a habit of doing this, it can get out of hand. Before you know it, they're borrowing from their escrow account and cannot repay the money. At that point, they start using new escrow deposits to pay off the old ones, and now you have a classic case of a Ponzi scheme

This is fraud, plain and simple, and will ultimately put the principal in jail.

Unfortunately, this has happened a lot lately. Here are some examples below:

Fraudulent Title Company

In one situation, a title agent was accused of stealing millions of dollars in customer escrow funds, taking the money to Las Vegas, and going on a gambling spree. The title insurance underwriter conducted an audit and discovered discrepancies in this company's escrow account and took action against the title services company. Fraud detectives determined that the owner of the title company had misappropriated funds in excess of $1 million from a specific escrow account, and used the money to buy vehicles, travel, and even make a down payment on a multi-million-dollar land purchase. The owner's title agent license was immediately revoked, and she faces up to sixty years in prison if convicted.

Fraudulent Attorney

In another example, a title and closing attorney and owner of a title services company surrendered to the county authorities for issuing a forged instrument, grand theft, mortgage fraud, and misappropriating monies. This attorney had failed to satisfy mortgages in at least two refinance closings, and had failed to place title insurance.

This led to one homeowner losing her home when the attorney failed to pay off her mortgage without informing her. The title insurance through his company had been cancelled, while he forged letters to secure refinances. This attorney's license was revoked.

Fraudulent Title Company

In another case, a husband and wife were indicted by a federal grand jury for defrauded companies and individuals out of over $5 million. This pair owned a title company that held money in escrow, and stole money from that escrow account to cover company and personal expenses. The pair transferred money out of the escrow account without permission, and without completing the transaction paperwork required by law.

Fraudulent Title Company

A licensed insurance escrow agent pled guilty to engaging in Organized Criminal Activity, a 1st degree felony. This escrow officer devised a multi-million dollar mortgage fraud scheme and with the help of others, defrauded buyers, sellers, and lenders to sign or execute real estate settlement documents and money transfers affecting real property in the amount of over $2 million. The scheme involved fraudulent representations by real estate investors who along with the escrow agent purchased several homes at below market prices. They recruited non-suspecting customers who believed they were purchasing the properties from the builders at a great price when in fact they were paying more for the houses then the builder was selling them for.

Fraudulent Loan Officer

A former bank loan officer pleaded guilty to helping clients in their real estate flipping fraud. In indictments, parties involved were accused of perpetuating false information on actual sale prices, sellers and buyers and down payment sources as they resold properties at inflated prices. This happened over several years resulting in defaulting on more than $100 million in loans.

Fraudulent Title Company

At title agency pleaded guilty in federal court to one count of wire fraud and one count of insurance fraud after embezzling more than $2 million from clients. The title agent commingled and transferred millions of dollars between clients.

Fraudulent Realtor and Title Company

A licensed real estate salesperson and insurance agent who worked for a title and real estate service company engaged in a pattern of insurance/mortgage fraud using proceeds intended for mortgage insurance or title insurance. They misappropriated, converted and embezzled more than $220,000 in proceeds by issuing checks for their own benefit from trust and title insurance accounts. They were charged with five counts of theft, three counts of theft by swindle, eight counts of insurance fraud and one count of racketeering.

Fraudulent Mortgage Company

The owner of a mortgage company and their loan processor knowingly facilitated a large-scale mortgage fraud scheme with other defendants. The defendants found "straw buyers" to purchase residential property, offering them several thousand for each property that they purchased. They used their parents to purchase over 10+ properties as straw buyers. The mortgage company withheld information from the mortgage lender and allowed the loans to be processed. They opened title insurance policies to protect the purchaser and lender on the mortgages, which subsequently were defaulted. Both defendants were charged with two counts of mortgage fraud.

Fraudulent Title Company

A title company owner was charged with using his position as president to switch funds illegally between two title companies and to take escrow funds--customers' money held as collateral in special bank accounts--for his own use, including purchases of country club memberships, stocks, bonds and stereo equipment. He was also charged with forging signatures on documents certifying the companies' financial condition.

The Department of Financial Services

The Department of Financial Services licenses title agents and agencies and enforces licensing provisions. They may investigate title agents and agencies, and may impose a variety of sanctions if it determines that they've violated state law or department rules. Most often, investigations result from complaints filed with the department. These complaints typically involve failure to pay fees, escrow disputes, rebating violations, unlicensed activity, and fraudulent or deceptive practices. The department also opens investigations for agents and agencies that fail to pay the required annual administrative surcharge.

The staff of the department's Bureau of Investigation conducts all investigations. If the investigation determines that grounds exist, the department can fine, suspend, or revoke an agent or agency license. In Fiscal Year 2007 to 2008, the department reported investigating 320 title insurance complaints, and spent $781,719 on title insurance investigations and enforcement activities. Of these investigations, sixty-three resulted in license suspension, twenty resulted in license revocation, and thirty-eight resulted in probation, fines, and/or cease and desist orders.

The Office of Insurance Regulation licenses title insurers and enforces licensing provisions. Title insurers provide the financial guarantee behind title policies and as a result, the state seeks to ensure that the companies can meet their legal obligations. The Office of Insurance Regulation has three general responsibilities for such insurers: licensing insurers and ensuring company solvency, taking enforcement actions when it detects violations of regulatory requirements, and setting rates for title insurance premiums.

The office also issues certificates of authority to insurance companies conducting insurance transactions in Florida. The Uniform Certificate of Authority Application requires the filing of the articles of incorporation, bylaws, plan of operation, biographical information, and background checks on all company officers. Insurers must also file financial data to confirm compliance with statutory requirements and solvency. Applicants for a certificate of authority must pay an application fee of $1,500 and an annual fee of $1,000 thereafter.

In addition to licensing fees, title insurers must pay an annual administrative surcharge of $200 for each agency appointed to represent their company, and for each retail office they operate. Surcharge revenues are deposited into the Insurance Regulatory Trust Fund, and may be used to defray the cost of regulatory activities such as audits, statistical gathering, and rate setting. Insurers must also pay a premium tax to the Department of Revenue on the gross amount of premiums sold in the state. State law requires insurers to remit a 1.75 percent premium tax on the amount of the premium.

While insurers submit the taxes to the Department of Revenue, the Office of Insurance Regulation can audit the companies to ensure that they pay the appropriate taxes. The office also conducts investigations and takes enforcement actions when it detects apparent violations of statutory requirements.

From 2003 to 2012, the office opened eleven investigations involving eight title insurers. These investigations focused on insurer activities involving reinsurance, commissions, contracts, rebating, and affiliated business arrangements, and included allegations of illegal inducements, inappropriate rebates, and fraud.

The bottom line is: know your title company and know who you're dealing with. Don't use the bank's title company. Establish a relationship with a title company whose principals are individuals that you trust and have a relationship with. This will build good will and trust in your relationship, and you'll be able to negotiate better closing costs for future transactions.

Chapter 23

Seven Title Insurance Tips & Secrets

Secret #1 – Simultaneous Policies

If you buy a house and get an owner's title policy for $100,000, and you obtain financing to buy the house, the lender will require their own title insurance policy. This policy is called a simultaneous policy, which means that you pay full price for the owner's policy and you get the simultaneous policy for a promulgated rate of only $25. Many title companies increase the cost from $25 to $250 or more. Knowing this tip can save you hundreds of dollars at every closing.

Secret #2 – Promulgated Rate

Title insurance promulgated rates are title insurance premiums a title company is allowed to charge. That is, the state sets a minimum rate and title companies have to charge a rate that is the same or higher than this promulgated rate. It would benefit you to know what the state's promulgated rate is, in order to see how much you're being charged over the minimum rate. Know what the promulgated rate is in your state, and don't pay more than this minimum rate.

As a title company, we believe that charging more than this rate is not justified for our clients. Unfortunately, not all settlement agents feel the same way. Closing costs vary substantially. That's why the new RESPA laws were established in order to make the market more competitive and fair for the consumer.

Secret #3 – Escrow Agreements and Deposits

You should always use an escrow agreement that stipulates, in the event of a default by one party, what the procedure and instructions are for the title company or attorney, and how they should manage the escrow dispute and release of the escrow deposit.

When you receive proof of deposit from your buyers, you want to make sure that the title company has received cleared good funds into their escrow account. For this reason, you should make sure that all deposits are in cleared funds only. Try not to accept personal checks if you don't know the buyer and/or if their funds will clear. A stop-payment can be issued on cashier's checks or printed fraudulently. It's best to insist on a wire transfer in order to ensure that the deposits are cleared funds. The same applies to the funds required for closing. Always use wire transfers if you want to be safe.

Secret #4 – Reissue Rate Credit

If the seller can give to the title company a policy that was issued in the past three years, then the title company can provide a reissue rate at a substantial savings. Always ask the seller if they have a copy of their original title insurance policy, if they purchased the property in the previous three years. You can receive this reissue rate credit for your new owner's title policy. The actual amount of the credit is the same amount, regardless of whether the policy is one, two, or three years old. If the policy is older than three years, then you won't be able to receive the reissue credit.

In the case of a refinance, you can get a reissue credit if you can provide a copy of your owner's title policy, regardless of when you purchased the property. It's imperative that you store your title policy in a safe and secure place.

Secret #5 – Can You Prepare Your Own Deed?

A common issue that we see when it comes to title examination is the use of deeds that are purchased at the local store.

178

While these deeds are valid and can be used, you need to keep a few things in mind.

When you first purchase a property, you are taking legal title. Why would you jeopardize your equitable interest in the property by preparing a fill-in-the-blank document from the local store? There are many title companies and attorneys that would prepare a deed for a minimal expense. This is especially true if you have an existing relationship with them.

Should you decide to prepare one of these deeds yourself, please keep a few items in mind. In Florida, all deeds should include the name of the grantor (seller) and grantee (buyer). Deeds should include the marital status of all parties. The complete legal description and parcel identification number should also be included. Please do not copy the legal description from the county property appraiser's office website, as this is usually an abbreviated version. Finally, make sure the deed contains a signature of the grantor (seller), two witnesses, and a notary.

Secret #6 – Controlled Business Arrangements

A Controlled Business Arrangement is where a bank, real estate agent, mortgage broker, or title company has an agreement with the other to provide their services to their clients for a referral fee in return. While this is not illegal or necessarily unethical, you always want to ask the question, "Do you have a controlled business arrangement with anyone involved in this transaction?" This is especially important with real estate, because you want to make sure that your best interest is being protected.

Unfortunately, some individuals are more concerned about getting their referral fee as opposed to representing their client's best interests. Please note that it's a violation of Florida Bar regulations for an attorney to pay a referral fee to any person other than another attorney.

Secret #7 – Do you Interview your Title Company?

Do you interview your title company before you choose them for your closing? If not, then try and ask these questions the next time you have a closing:

- Ask them if they're experts in their field, or if they're a "middleman" company that refers their business out to another firm to issue your policy.
- Take a look at the company's name or website for a clue of whether they're a real company. There's so much fraud out there that you want to make sure you're dealing with a reputable company.
- Does the company have a database of satisfied, well-known customers, or just a list of anonymous "testimonials" that could have been written by anyone? Ask them to supply you with verifiable references. If they can't, chances are they don't want you to find out something they don't want you to know. I would suggest calling at least two of their customers to verify the company's integrity.
- Will they actually follow through on your transaction, or will they just skip town, leaving you to start at the beginning? Are they ethical and do they implement world-class business practices? Do they have an actual phone number that dials through to a live person?

Make sure that any title agency you're considering is licensed. You can check by visiting their website MyFloridaCFO.com, or by calling the Florida Department of Financial Services Consumer Helpline toll-free at 1-877-MY-FL-CFO (1-877-693-5236). If you're dealing with an attorney, contact the Florida Bar Association to determine whether they're a member at (800) 342-8060 or www.floridabar.org.

SUMMARY

I hope that you've enjoyed reading *The Title Wave of Real Estate* as much as I enjoyed researching and writing it. If you can only remember a few things from this book, please remember the following important items:

- Always get a title insurance policy for all transactions especially for simultaneous or double closings.
- Always obtain title to a property using a warranty type deed.
- Always choose your own title company because you have the legal right to do so.
- Always review the title commitment several days before and at the closing.
- Always inquire about any requirements on Schedule B-I that are not clear to you.
- Always review the municipal lien search in full for any permit or code issues.
- Always ask questions if you don't understand something throughout your closing process. In some cases you may decide to hire an attorney to represent you.
- Always review and never sign your closing documents until you've reviewed all of the above.

Please join me at the local real estate meetings that I attend in South Florida, on the first Tuesday first Wednesday and second Thursday of each month. I love working in real estate, and I really enjoy speaking on the topic of real estate, so please make sure to introduce yourself.

If you enjoyed reading this book and would like to share your positive feedback and thoughts, I would be very happy to post your positive testimonials on my website.

I hope that you choose *Independence Title* for your next closing, and I hope that you have learned something useful from this book that will help you save some money on your next real estate closing. Finally, remember to watch out for potential problems at your next closing to protect yourself from any costly real estate transactions!

I wish you good luck and great success as a homebuyer, home seller, real estate investor or real estate professional.

Kevin Tacher, Founder & CEO
Amazon.com Best-Selling Author
Independence Title, Inc.
4700 W Prospect Rd, Suite 115
Fort Lauderdale, FL 33309
Phone: 954-335-9305
Email: Kevin@TitleRate.com
Web: www.TitleRate.com

TitleRate.com is the leading source for title insurance rates, real estate mobile applications, and up to date real estate information and education.